LYNN RUTLEDGE

LIGHT FOR EACH DAY

DAILY DEVOTIONS CONTAINING
ONLY THE WORDS OF THE BIBLE | VOLUME 2

REDWOOD GROVE PUBLISHING

LIGHT FOR EACH DAY, VOLUME 2
PUBLISHED BY REDWOOD GROVE PUBLISHING

Cover design: Brian Montes

Interior design: Chris Gilbert, Studio Gearbox

ISBN-10: 0989705811

ISBN-13: 978-0-9897058-1-3

The publisher can be contacted at RedwoodGrovePublishing@gmail.com.

Send out your light and your truth;
let them lead me.

PSALM 43:3 (ESV)

WAYS TO READ THIS BOOK

You can follow the calendar dates and read one page daily.
This volume covers July 1 through December 31.

OR

You can follow the day numbers (DAY 1, etc.)
and read on your own schedule.

OR

You can use this as a school year devotional and read one page each school day for approximately a nine-month school year, following the day numbers.

ABOUT THIS BOOK

All the words of *Light for Each Day* are quoted directly from the Bible. A few words have been replaced for clarity (such as "God" in place of "he"). These are indicated by brackets.

A line break in the text indicates a new scripture reference. The references are listed at the bottom of each page.

Each day's reading uses verses from only one Bible version, which is noted at the end of the list of scripture references.

The readings titled "God Speaks" and/or "Jesus Speaks" contain only verses directly quoting God or Jesus as recorded in the Bible. There is one of these each week.

At least one reading each week is a prayer.

Volume One and *Volume Two* combined contain verses from all 66 books of the Bible.

The LORD Has Done Great Things for Us

The LORD is God,
and he has made his light shine on us.

For God, who said, "Let light shine out of darkness," made his light shine in our hearts to give us the light of the knowledge of God's glory displayed in the face of Christ.

He has rescued us from the dominion of darkness and brought us into the kingdom of the Son he loves.

He saved us, not because of righteous things we had done, but because of his mercy.

He has given us new birth into a living hope through the resurrection of Jesus Christ from the dead.

God has given us eternal life, and this life is in his Son.

God...has blessed us in the heavenly realms with every spiritual blessing in Christ.

He has given us his very great and precious promises.

He anointed us, set his seal of ownership on us, and put his Spirit in our hearts as a deposit, guaranteeing what is to come.

The LORD has done great things for us,
and we are filled with joy.

Ps. 118:27; 2 Cor. 4:6; Col. 1:13; Titus 3:5; 1 Pet. 1:3; 1 John 5:11; Eph. 1:3; 2 Pet. 1:4; 2 Cor. 1:21-22; Ps. 126:3 (All verses are from the NIV.)

GOD SPEAKS:

Promises for My People

I will save my people,

the people whom I formed for myself
  that they might declare my praise,

everyone who is called by my name,
  whom I created for my glory.

My dwelling place shall be with them.

They shall all know me, from the least of them to the greatest.

Before they call I will answer;
  while they are yet speaking I will hear.

They shall...dwell beneath my shadow;
  they shall flourish like the grain;
they shall blossom like the vine.

Their life shall be like a watered garden.

They shall be fruitful and multiply.

They shall dwell securely, and none shall make them afraid.

Behold, my servants shall eat...
  my servants shall drink...
my servants shall rejoice...
  my servants shall sing for gladness of heart.

And my people shall be satisfied with my goodness.

Zech. 8:7; Is. 43:21; Is. 43:7; Ezek. 37:27; Jer. 31:34; Is. 65:24; Hos. 14:7; Jer. 31:12; Jer. 23:3;
Ezek. 34:28; Is. 65:13-14; Jer. 31:14 (All verses are from the ESV.)

My Hope

I know whom I have believed, and I am convinced that he is able to guard until that Day what has been entrusted to me.

My hope is from him.

Surely my right is with the Lord,
  and my recompense with my God.

God will ransom my soul from the power of Sheol,
  for he will receive me.

The Lord will rescue me from every evil deed and bring me safely into his heavenly kingdom.

He will bring me out to the light;
  I shall look upon his vindication.

God will let me look in triumph on my enemies.

My God in his steadfast love will meet me.

For I know that my Redeemer lives,
  and at the last he will stand upon the earth.
And after my skin has been thus destroyed,
  yet in my flesh I shall see God,
whom I shall see for myself...
  My heart faints within me!

For now we see in a mirror dimly, but then face to face. Now I know in part; then I shall know fully, even as I have been fully known.

Then my soul will rejoice in the Lord,
  exulting in his salvation.

And I shall dwell in the house of the Lord
  forever.

2 Tim. 1:12; Ps. 62:5; Is. 49:4; Ps. 49:15; 2 Tim. 4:18; Mic. 7:9; Ps. 59:10; Ps. 59:10; Job 19:25-27; 1 Cor. 13:12; Ps. 35:9; Ps. 23:6 (All verses are from the ESV.)

Profitable Investments

Buy truth, and do not sell it,
get wisdom and instruction and understanding.

Wisdom...is more precious than jewels;
and nothing you desire compares with her.

Godliness is profitable for all things, since it holds promise for the present life and also for the life to come.

Godliness actually is a means of great gain when accompanied by contentment.

Serve the LORD with all your heart. You must not turn aside, for then you would go after futile things which can not profit or deliver.

Do not store up for yourselves treasures on earth.

Riches do not profit in the day of wrath.

For what will it profit a man if he gains the whole world and forfeits his soul?

But store up for yourselves treasures in heaven,

true riches.

For where your treasure is, there your heart will be also.

How blessed is the man who finds wisdom
and the man who gains understanding.
For her profit is better than the profit of silver
and her gain better than fine gold.

Prov. 23:23; Prov. 3:13, 15; 1 Tim. 4:8; 1 Tim. 6:6; 1 Sam. 12:20-21; Matt. 6:19; Prov. 11:4; Matt. 16:26; Matt. 6:20; Luke 16:11; Matt 6:21; Prov. 3:13-14 (All verses are from the NASB.)

I Walk in Your Faithfulness

O Lord...your steadfast love is before my eyes,
 and I walk in your faithfulness.

Even though I walk through the valley of the shadow of death,
 I will fear no evil,
for you are with me.

Though I walk in the midst of trouble,
 you preserve my life.

You will not restrain
 your mercy from me;
your steadfast love and your faithfulness will
 ever preserve me!

For you have delivered my soul from death,
 yes, my feet from falling,
that I may walk...
 in the light of life.

When I thought, "My foot slips,"
 your steadfast love, O Lord, held me up.

You gave a wide place for my steps under me,
 and my feet did not slip.

Your word is a lamp to my feet
 and a light to my path.

Lead me in the path of your commandments,
 for I delight in it.

Preserve me from violent men,
 who have planned to trip up my feet.

Keep steady my steps according to your promise.

Ps. 26:2-3; Ps. 23:4; Ps. 138:7; Ps. 40:11; Ps. 56:13; Ps. 94:18; 2 Sam. 22:37; Ps. 119:105;
Ps. 119:35; Ps. 140:4; Ps. 119:133 (All verses are from the ESV.)

Hold Fast

Take hold of the eternal life, to which you were called.

Take hold of the life that really is life.

Take good care...to love the LORD your God, to walk in all his ways, to keep his commandments, and to hold fast to him.

Hate what is evil, hold fast to what is good.

Hold fast to love and justice.

Do not let loyalty and faithfulness forsake you;
   bind them around your neck,
write them on the tablet of your heart.

Let us hold fast to what we have attained.

Let us hold fast to the confession of our hope without wavering, for he who has promised is faithful.

For we have become partners of Christ, if only we hold our first confidence firm to the end.

Do not...abandon that confidence of yours; it brings a great reward.

Hold fast to the LORD your God, as you have done to this day.

Keep yourselves in the love of God; look forward to the mercy of our Lord Jesus Christ that leads to eternal life.

These are the words of the Son of God..."Only hold fast to what you have until I come."

1 Tim. 6:12; 1 Tim. 6:19; Josh 22:5; Rom. 12:9; Hos. 12:6; Prov. 3:3; Phil. 3:16; Heb. 10:23; Heb. 3:14; Heb. 10:35; Josh. 23:8; Jude 1:21; Rev. 2:18, 25 (All verses are from the NRSV.)

Unity in Christ

All of you who were baptized into Christ have clothed yourselves with Christ....
You are all one in Christ Jesus.

You are a chosen race....You once were not a people, but now you are the people
of God.

There is no distinction between Greek and Jew, circumcised and uncircumcised,
barbarian, Scythian, slave and freeman.

There is neither male nor female.

But Christ is all, and in all.

Preserve the unity of the Spirit in the bond of peace. There is one body and one
Spirit, just as also you were called in one hope of your calling; one Lord, one
faith, one baptism, one God and Father of all.

You are all sons of God through faith in Christ Jesus.

You are all brothers.

Behold, how good and how pleasant it is
    for brothers to dwell together in unity!

All of you be harmonious, sympathetic, brotherly,

having been knit together in love.

May...God...grant you to be of the same mind with one another according to
Christ Jesus, so that with one accord you may with one voice glorify the God
and Father of our Lord Jesus Christ.

The fellowship of the Holy Spirit be with you all.

Gal. 3:27-28; 1 Pet. 2:9-10; Col. 3:11; Gal. 3:28; Col. 3:11; Eph. 4:3-6; Gal. 3:26; Matt. 23:8;
Ps. 133:1; 1 Pet. 3:8; Col. 2:2; Rom. 15:5-6; 2 Cor. 13:14 (All verses are from the NASB.)

Meaningful Work

What do people get in this life for all their hard work and anxiety? Their days of labor are filled with pain and grief; even at night their minds cannot rest. It is all meaningless.

All their hard work is for nothing—like working for the wind. Throughout their lives, they live under a cloud—frustrated, discouraged, and angry.

We all come to the end of our lives as naked and empty-handed as on the day we were born. We can't take our riches with us.

If there is no resurrection, "Let's feast and drink, for tomorrow we die!"

But in fact, Christ has been raised from the dead. He is the first of a great harvest of all who have died.

Indeed, the time is coming when all the dead in their graves...will rise again. Those who have done good will rise to experience eternal life.

God paid a ransom to save you from the empty life you inherited from your ancestors.

There is hope for your future.

Work willingly at whatever you do, as though you were working for the Lord rather than for people. Remember that the Lord will give you an inheritance as your reward, and that the Master you are serving is Christ.

Make the most of every opportunity in these evil days. Don't act thought-lessly, but understand what the Lord wants you to do. Don't be drunk with wine, because that will ruin your life. Instead, be filled with the Holy Spirit.

Be strong and courageous, for your work will be rewarded.

Always work enthusiastically for the Lord, for you know that nothing you do for the Lord is ever useless.

Eccl. 2:22-23; Eccl. 5:16-17; Eccl. 5:15; 1 Cor. 15:32; 1 Cor. 15:20; John 5:28-29; 1 Pet. 1:18; Jer. 31:17; Col. 3:23-24; Eph. 5:16-18; 2 Chr. 15:7; 1 Cor. 15:58 (All verses are from the NLT.)

GOD SPEAKS:

Do Not Fear

Thus says the LORD,
  he who created you, O Jacob,
he who formed you, O Israel:
  Do not fear, for I have redeemed you;
I have called you by name, you are mine.

I, I am he who comforts you;
  why then are you afraid of a mere mortal who must die,
a human being who fades like grass?
  You have forgotten the LORD, your Maker,
who stretched out the heavens
  and laid the foundations of the earth.

Listen to me, you who know righteousness,
  you people who have my teaching in your hearts;
do not fear the reproach of others,
  and do not be dismayed when they revile you.
For the moth will eat them up like a garment,
  and the worm will eat them like wool;
but my deliverance will be forever,
  and my salvation to all generations.

I, the LORD your God,
  hold your right hand;
it is I who say to you, "Do not fear,
  I will help you."

Call on me in the day of trouble;
  I will deliver you, and you shall glorify me.

Do not be afraid....I am your shield.

I will be with you; I will not fail you or forsake you....I hereby command you:
Be strong and courageous; do not be frightened or dismayed.

Is. 43:1; Is. 51:12-13; Is. 51:7-8; Is. 41:13; Ps. 50:15; Gen. 15:1; Josh. 1:5, 9 (All verses are from
the NRSV.)

Forever

Though the wicked sprout like grass
  and all evildoers flourish,
they are doomed to destruction forever.

But whoever does the will of God abides forever.

His saints...are preserved forever.

As the mountains surround Jerusalem,
  so the LORD surrounds his people,
from this time forth and forevermore.

He will swallow up death forever.

The saints of the Most High shall receive the kingdom and possess the kingdom forever, forever and ever.

And the LORD will reign over them in Mount Zion
  from this time forth and forevermore.

Then justice will dwell in the wilderness,
  and righteousness abide in the fruitful field.
And the effect of righteousness will be peace,
  and the result of righteousness, quietness and trust forever.

Steadfast love will be built up forever.

Then the righteous will shine like the sun in the kingdom.

Those who are wise shall shine like the brightness of the sky above; and those who turn many to righteousness, like the stars forever and ever.

Ps. 92:7; 1 John 2:17; Ps. 37:28; Ps. 125:2; Is. 25:8; Dan. 7:18; Mic. 4:7; Is. 32:16-17; Ps. 89:2; Matt. 13:43; Dan. 12:3 (All verses are from the ESV.)

The LORD Will Be Your Confidence

You are God's people.

You are blessed, because the Spirit of glory and of God rests upon you.

Your sins are forgiven for [Jesus'] name's sake.

And you have overcome the evil one.

You are strong.

The joy of the LORD is your strength.

You stand firm in your faith.

For he who is in you is greater than he who is in the world.

[He] will sustain you to the end, guiltless.

You will walk on your way securely.

The LORD will keep you from all evil;
  he will keep your life.

You will not fear the terror of the night,
  nor the arrow that flies by day,
nor the pestilence that stalks in darkness,
  nor the destruction that wastes at noonday.

If you lie down, you will not be afraid;
  when you lie down, your sleep will be sweet.

For the LORD will be your confidence.

1 Pet. 2:10; 1 Pet. 4:14; 1 John 2:12; 1 John 2:14; 1 John 2:14; Neh. 8:10; 2 Cor. 1:24; 1 John 4:4;
1 Cor. 1:8; Prov. 3:23; Ps. 121:7; Ps. 91:5-6; Prov. 3:24; Prov. 3:26 (All verses are from the ESV.)

I Wait for You

O my God, make haste to help me!

For you are the God of my salvation;
   for you I wait all day long.

From ages past no one has heard,
   no ear has perceived,
no eye has seen any God besides you,
   who works for those who wait for him.

I call upon you, for you will answer me, O God;
   incline your ear to me, hear my words.

O guard my life, and deliver me;
   do not let me be put to shame, for I take refuge in you.
May integrity and uprightness preserve me,
   for I wait for you.

O my strength, I will watch for you;
   for you, O God, are my fortress.

You, O Lord, are my hope.

I will hope continually,
   and will praise you yet more and more.

I cry to you, O Lord...
   You will deal bountifully with me.

In the morning you hear my voice;
   in the morning I plead my case to you, and watch.

My prayer is to you, O Lord.
   At an acceptable time, O God,
in the abundance of your steadfast love, answer me.

Ps. 71:12; Ps. 25:5; Is. 64:4; Ps. 17:6; Ps. 25:20-21; Ps. 59:9; Ps. 71:5; Ps. 71:14; Ps. 142:5, 7; Ps. 5:3; Ps. 69:13 (All verses are from the NRSV.)

Peace from God

The LORD gives his people strength.
   The LORD blesses them with peace.

But there is no peace for the wicked.

Letting your sinful nature control your mind leads to death. But letting the Spirit control your mind leads to life and peace.

Don't copy the behavior and customs of this world, but let God transform you into a new person by changing the way you think.

Throw off your old sinful nature and your former way of life, which is corrupted by lust and deception. Instead, let the Spirit renew your thoughts and attitudes.

Fix your thoughts on what is true, and honorable, and right, and pure, and lovely, and admirable. Think about things that are excellent and worthy of praise. Keep putting into practice all you learned and received from me— everything you heard from me and saw me doing. Then the God of peace will be with you.

Don't worry about anything; instead, pray about everything. Tell God what you need, and thank him for all he has done. Then you will experience God's peace, which exceeds anything we can understand. His peace will guard your hearts and minds as you live in Christ Jesus.

I pray that God...will fill you completely with joy and peace because you trust in him.

For the Kingdom of God is...goodness and peace and joy in the Holy Spirit.

May the Lord of peace himself give you his peace at all times and in every situation.

Ps. 29:11; Is. 48:22; Rom. 8:6; Rom. 12:2; Eph. 4:22-23; Phil. 4:8-9; Phil. 4:6-7; Rom. 15:13; Rom. 14:17; 2 Thess. 3:16 (All verses are from the NLT.)

My Life in Christ

Even before I was born, God chose me and called me by his marvelous grace. Then it pleased him to reveal his Son to me.

I was blind, and now I can see!

God had mercy on me.

Oh, how generous and gracious our Lord was! He filled me with the faith and love that come from Christ Jesus.

I no longer count on my own righteousness through obeying the law; rather, I become righteous through faith in Christ.

May I never boast about anything except the cross of our Lord Jesus Christ. Because of that cross, my interest in this world has been crucified, and the world's interest in me has also died.

My old self has been crucified with Christ. It is no longer I who live, but Christ lives in me. So I live in this earthly body by trusting in the Son of God, who loved me and gave himself for me.

I want to know Christ and experience the mighty power that raised him from the dead.

Everything else is worthless when compared with the infinite value of knowing Christ Jesus my Lord. For his sake I have discarded everything else, counting it all as garbage, so that I could gain Christ and become one with him.

I want to suffer with him, sharing in his death, so that one way or another I will experience the resurrection from the dead!

For to me, living means living for Christ, and dying is even better.

Gal. 1:15-16; John 9:25; 1 Tim. 1:13; 1 Tim. 1:14; Phil. 3:9; Gal. 6:14; Gal. 2:20; Phil. 3:10; Phil. 3:8-9; Phil. 3:10-11; Phil. 1:21 (All verses are from the NLT.)

Only God Can Save

Do not put your trust in princes,
  in human beings, who cannot save.

In the LORD alone
  are deliverance and strength.

For who is God besides the LORD?
  And who is the Rock except our God?

Cursed is the one who trusts in man,
  who draws strength from mere flesh
and whose heart turns away from the LORD.

Woe to those who go down to Egypt for help,
  who rely on horses,
who trust in the multitude of their chariots
  and in the great strength of their horsemen,
but do not look to the Holy One of Israel,
  or seek help from the LORD...
The Egyptians are mere mortals and not God;
  their horses are flesh and not spirit.

No king is saved by the size of his army;
  no warrior escapes by his great strength.
A horse is a vain hope for deliverance;
  despite all its great strength it cannot save.
But the eyes of the LORD are on those who fear him,
  on those whose hope is in his unfailing love,
to deliver them from death.

Some trust in chariots and some in horses,
  but we trust in the name of the LORD our God.

Ps. 146:3; Is. 45:24; 2 Sam. 22:32; Jer. 17:5; Is. 31:1, 3; Ps. 33:16-19; Ps. 20:7 (All verses are from the NIV.)

Water for the Thirsty

Blessed are those who...thirst for righteousness, for they shall be satisfied.

When the poor and needy seek water,
   and there is none,
and their tongue is parched with thirst,
   I the LORD will answer them;
I the God of Israel will not forsake them.
   I will open rivers on the bare heights,
and fountains in the midst of the valleys.
   I will make the wilderness a pool of water,
and the dry land springs of water.

For I will pour water on the thirsty land,
   and streams on the dry ground;
I will pour my Spirit upon your offspring,
   and my blessing on your descendants.

To the thirsty I will give from the spring of the water of life.

Whoever drinks of the water that I will give him will never be thirsty again.
The water that I will give him will become in him a spring of water welling up
to eternal life.

Whoever believes in me, as the Scripture has said, "Out of his heart will flow
rivers of living water."

If anyone thirsts, let him come to me and drink.

Come, everyone who thirsts,
   come to the waters.

Matt. 5:6; Is. 41:17-18; Is. 44:3; Rev. 21:6; John 4:14; John 7:38; John 7:37; Is. 55:1 (All verses
are from the ESV.)

Jesus Suffered as We Do

Since [God's] children have flesh and blood, [Jesus] too shared in their humanity so that by his death he might break the power of him who holds the power of death—that is, the devil—and free those who all their lives were held in slavery by their fear of death.

He had to be made like them, fully human in every way, in order that he might become a merciful and faithful high priest in service to God, and that he might make atonement for the sins of the people.

Surely he took up our pain
   and bore our suffering.

He was despised and rejected by mankind,
   a man of suffering, and familiar with pain.

Jesus wept.

During the days of Jesus' life on earth, he offered up prayers and petitions with fervent cries and tears.

Being in anguish, he prayed...earnestly, and his sweat was like drops of blood falling to the ground.

Christ suffered in his body.

He was pierced for our transgressions,
   he was crushed for our iniquities...
He was oppressed and afflicted.

He was crucified.

But we...see Jesus, who was made lower than the angels for a little while, now crowned with glory and honor because he suffered death, so that by the grace of God he might taste death for everyone. In bringing many sons and daughters to glory, it was fitting that God...should make the pioneer of their salvation perfect through what he suffered.

Heb. 2:14-15; Heb. 2:17; Is. 53:4; Is. 53:3; John 11:35; Heb. 5:7; Luke 22:44; 1 Pet. 4:1; Is. 53:5, 7; 2 Cor. 13:4; Heb. 2:9-10 (All verses are from the NIV.)

The Universe's Existence

By faith we understand that the universe was created by the word of God, so that what is seen was not made out of things that are visible.

He spoke, and it came to be;
   he commanded, and it stood firm.

God said, "Let there be light," and there was light.

It is he who made the earth by his power,
   who established the world by his wisdom,
and by his understanding stretched out the heavens,

who spread out the earth and what comes from it,
   who gives breath to the people on it
and spirit to those who walk in it.

There is one God, the Father, from whom are all things and for whom we exist, and one Lord, Jesus Christ, through whom are all things and through whom we exist.

In the beginning was the Word, and the Word was with God, and the Word was God. He was in the beginning with God. All things were made through him, and without him was not any thing made that was made.

For by [Jesus] all things were created, in heaven and on earth, visible and invisible, whether thrones or dominions or rulers or authorities—all things were created through him and for him.

And he is before all things, and in him all things hold together.

He upholds the universe by the word of his power.

Heb. 11:3; Ps. 33:9; Gen. 1:3; Jer. 10:12; Is. 42:5; 1 Cor. 8:6; John 1:1-3; Col. 1:16; Col. 1:17; Heb. 1:3 (All verses are from the ESV.)

LORD, Forgive Us

LORD, if you kept a record of our sins,
  who, O Lord, could ever survive?

For our sins...testify against us.

We have rebelled against you and scorned your commands and regulations.

Our sins are piled higher than our heads, and our guilt has reached to the
heavens.

We are all infected and impure with sin.
  When we display our righteous deeds,
they are nothing but filthy rags.

But you offer forgiveness,
  that we might learn to fear you.

O Lord, you are so good, so ready to forgive.

Where is another God like you,
  who pardons the guilt of the remnant,
overlooking the sins of his special people?
  ...Once again you will have compassion on us.
You will trample our sins under your feet
  and throw them into the depths of the ocean!

Have mercy on us, LORD, have mercy.

Forgive us our sins,
  as we have forgiven those who sin against us.

Show us your unfailing love, O LORD.

Restore us again, O God of our salvation...
  revive us again.

Ps. 130:3; Is. 59:12; Dan. 9:5; Ezra 9:6; Is. 64:6; Ps. 130:4; Ps. 86:5; Mic. 7:18-19; Ps. 123:3;
Matt. 6:12; Ps. 85:7; Ps. 85:4, 6 (All verses are from the NLT.)

Freed from the Law

When we were in the flesh, the sinful passions operated through the law in every part of us and bore fruit for death.

We...were in slavery under the elemental forces of the world.

But now we have been released from the law.

The law was given through Moses;
  grace and truth came through Jesus Christ.

God sent His Son...to redeem those under the law.

He erased the certificate of debt, with its obligations, that was against us and opposed to us, and has taken it out of the way by nailing it to the cross.

Therefore, no condemnation now exists for those in Christ Jesus.

We may serve in the new way of the Spirit and not in the old letter of the law.

The Spirit's law of life in Christ Jesus has set you free from the law of sin and of death.

For the letter kills, but the Spirit produces life.

Where the Spirit of the Lord is, there is freedom.

In the past, when you didn't know God, you were enslaved to things that by nature are not gods. But now, since you know God, or rather have become known by God, how can you turn back again to the weak and bankrupt elemental forces? Do you want to be enslaved to them all over again?

Christ has liberated us to be free. Stand firm then and don't submit again to a yoke of slavery.

Rom. 7:5; Gal. 4:3; Rom. 7:6; John 1:17; Gal. 4:4-5; Col. 2:14; Rom. 8:1; Rom. 7:6; Rom. 8:2; 2 Cor. 3:6; 2 Cor. 3: 17; Gal. 4:8-9; Gal. 5:1 (All verses are from the HCSB.)

Idols

Keep away from anything that might take God's place in your hearts.

Idols are worthless; they are ridiculous lies!

But the LORD is the only true God.
  He is the living God.

Be careful. Don't let your heart be deceived so that you turn away from the LORD.

Don't go back to worshiping worthless idols that cannot help or rescue you—
they are totally useless!

You must worship the LORD your God
  and serve only him.

For the LORD your God is a devouring fire; he is a jealous God.

You must love the LORD your God with all your heart, all your soul, all your
mind, and all your strength.

Troubles multiply for those who chase after other gods.

Those who worship false gods
  turn their backs on all God's mercies.

The LORD protects those who are loyal to him.

But those who trust in idols,
  who say, "You are our gods,"
will be turned away in shame.

My dear friends, flee from the worship of idols.

1 John 5:21; Jer. 10:15; Jer. 10:10; Deut. 11:16; 1 Sam. 12:21; Luke 4:8; Deut. 4:24; Mark 12:30;
Ps. 16:4; Jon. 2:8; Ps. 31:23; Is. 42:17; 1 Cor. 10:14 (All verses are from the NLT.)

Our Heavenly City

By faith Abraham, when called to go to a place he would later receive as his inheritance, obeyed and went, even though he did not know where he was going. By faith he made his home in the promised land like a stranger in a foreign country; he lived in tents, as did Isaac and Jacob, who were heirs with him of the same promise. For he was looking forward to the city with foundations, whose architect and builder is God.

We are foreigners and strangers...as were all our ancestors. Our days on earth are like a shadow.

For here we do not have an enduring city, but we are looking for the city that is to come,

the city of the living God, the heavenly Jerusalem.

Our citizenship is in heaven.

We fix our eyes not on what is seen, but on what is unseen, since what is seen is temporary, but what is unseen is eternal.

Look on Zion, the city of our festivals;
   your eyes will see Jerusalem,
a peaceful abode, a tent that will not be moved;
   its stakes will never be pulled up,
nor any of its ropes broken.

The throne of God and of the Lamb will be in the city, and his servants will serve him.

No one living in Zion will say, "I am ill";
   and the sins of those who dwell there will be forgiven.

On no day will its gates ever be shut, for there will be no night there.

And the name of the city...will be:
   THE LORD IS THERE.

Heb. 11:8-10; 1 Chr. 29:15; Heb. 13:14; Heb. 12:22; Phil. 3:20; 2 Cor. 4:18; Is. 33:20; Rev. 22:3; Is. 33:24; Rev. 21:25; Ezek. 48:35 (All verses are from the NIV.)

GOD SPEAKS:

My Plans for You

I know the plans I have for you, plans for your welfare and not for harm, to give you a future with hope.

With everlasting love I will have compassion on you.

I will...snap the bonds that bind you.

I will deliver you out of the hand of the wicked.

I will save you.

I will restore health to you,
   and your wounds I will heal.

I will comfort you.

A new heart I will give you, and a new spirit I will put within you.

I will welcome you,
   and I will be your father,
and you shall be my sons and daughters.

I will sprinkle clean water upon you, and you shall be clean.

I, I am He
   who blots out your transgressions for my own sake,
and I will not remember your sins.

I will make with you an everlasting covenant.

I will take you for my wife forever...in righteousness and in justice, in steadfast love, and in mercy.

I will indeed bless you.

And you shall know that I, the LORD, am your Savior.

Jer. 29:11; Is. 54:8; Nah. 1:13; Jer. 15:21; Zech. 8:13; Jer. 30:17; Is. 66:13; Ezek. 36:26; 2 Cor. 6:17-18; Ezek. 36:25; Is. 43:25; Is. 55:3; Hos. 2:19; Gen. 22:17; Is. 60:16 (All verses are from the NRSV.)

Christian Love

All of you share in God's grace with me.

I have you in my heart.

Night and day I constantly remember you in my prayers.

I thank my God every time I remember you.

In all my prayers for all of you, I always pray with joy because of your partnership in the gospel.

Your love has given me great joy and encouragement.

God can testify how I long for all of you with the affection of Christ Jesus.

I long to see you so that...you and I may be mutually encouraged by each other's faith.

Though I am absent from you in body, I am present with you in spirit and delight to see how disciplined you are and how firm your faith in Christ is.

My brothers and sisters, you whom I love and long for, my joy and crown, stand firm in the Lord...dear friends!

I urge you...to join me in my struggle by praying to God for me.

The grace of our Lord Jesus Christ be with your spirit, brothers and sisters.

My love to all of you in Christ Jesus. Amen.

Phil. 1:7; Phil. 1:7; 2 Tim.1:3; Phil. 1:3; Phil. 1:4-5; Philem. 1:7; Phil. 1:8; Rom. 1:11-12; Col. 2:5; Phil. 4:1; Rom. 15:30; Gal. 6:18; 1 Cor. 16:24 (All verses are from the NIV.)

Chosen by God

[God] has saved us and called us
  with a holy calling,
not according to our works,
  but according to His own purpose and grace,
which was given to us in Christ Jesus
  before time began.

For He chose us in Him, before the foundation of the world, to be holy and blameless in His sight.

He predestined us to be adopted through Jesus Christ for Himself, according to His favor and will.

For those He foreknew He also predestined to be conformed to the image of His Son, so that He would be the firstborn among many brothers.

And those He predestined, He also called; and those He called, He also justified; and those He justified, He also glorified.

By His own choice, He gave us a new birth by the message of truth so that we would be the firstfruits of His creatures,

appointed to eternal life.

We have also received an inheritance in Him, predestined according to the purpose of the One who works out everything in agreement with the decision of His will.

What then are we to say about these things?
  If God is for us, who is against us?

Who can bring an accusation against God's elect?
  God is the One who justifies.

For God did not appoint us to wrath, but to obtain salvation through our Lord Jesus Christ.

2 Tim. 1:9; Eph. 1:4; Eph. 1:5; Rom. 8:29; Rom. 8:30; James 1:18; Acts 13:48 ; Eph. 1:11; Rom. 8:31; Rom. 8:33; 1 Thess. 5:9 (All verses are from the HCSB.)

My Thoughts

You, O LORD, know me;
  You see me and test me.

You discern my thoughts from far away.

I remember the days of old,
  I think about all your deeds,
I meditate on the works of your hands.

Oh, how I love your law!
  It is my meditation all day long.

I will meditate on your precepts,
  and fix my eyes on your ways.
I will delight in your statutes;
  I will not forget your word.

When I think of your ways,
  I turn my feet to your decrees.

My soul is satisfied as with a rich feast,
  and my mouth praises you with joyful lips
when I think of you on my bed,
  and meditate on you in the watches of the night.

My eyes are awake before each watch of the night,
  that I may meditate on your promise.

Search me, O God, and know my heart;
  test me and know my thoughts.
See if there is any wicked way in me,
  and lead me in the way everlasting.

Let the...meditation of my heart
  be acceptable to you,
O LORD, my rock and my redeemer.

Jer. 12:3; Ps. 139:2; Ps. 143:5; Ps. 119:97; Ps. 119:15-16; Ps. 119:59; Ps. 63:5-6; Ps. 119:148;
Ps. 139:23-24; Ps. 19:14 (All verses are from the NRSV.)

Resisting Temptation

The grace of God has appeared...training us to renounce ungodliness and worldly passions, and to live self-controlled, upright, and godly lives.

No temptation has overtaken you that is not common to man. God is faithful, and he will not let you be tempted beyond your ability, but with the temptation he will also provide the way of escape, that you may be able to endure it.

Because [Jesus] himself has suffered when tempted, he is able to help those who are being tempted....For we do not have a high priest who is unable to sympathize with our weaknesses, but one who in every respect has been tempted as we are, yet without sin.

Be strong in the Lord and in the strength of his might.

Put on the whole armor of God, that you may be able to stand against the schemes of the devil. For we do not wrestle against flesh and blood, but against the rulers, against the authorities, against the cosmic powers over this present darkness, against the spiritual forces of evil in the heavenly places.

In all circumstances take up the shield of faith, with which you can extinguish all the flaming darts of the evil one. And take the helmet of salvation, and the sword of the Spirit, which is the word of God, praying at all times in the Spirit.

Do not be overcome by evil, but overcome evil with good.

Be sober-minded; be watchful. Your adversary the devil prowls around like a roaring lion, seeking someone to devour. Resist him, firm in your faith.

Submit yourselves...to God. Resist the devil, and he will flee from you.

Sin is crouching at the door. Its desire is for you, but you must rule over it.

For sin will have no dominion over you, since you are not under law but under grace.

Titus 2:11-12; 1 Cor. 10:13; Heb. 2:18, 4:15; Eph. 6:10; Eph. 6:11-12; Eph. 6:16-18; Rom. 12:21; 1 Pet. 5:8-9; James 4:7; Gen. 4:7; Rom. 6:14 (All verses are from the ESV.)

Rejoice

Happy are you, O Israel! Who is like you,
  a people saved by the LORD,
the shield of your help,
  and the sword of your triumph!

Shout, and sing for joy, O inhabitant of Zion,
  for great in your midst is the Holy One of Israel.

Rejoice in all the good that the LORD your God has given to you and to your house.

Be glad, O children of Zion,
  and rejoice in the LORD your God...
Praise the name of the LORD your God,
  who has dealt wondrously with you.

Rejoice in hope.

Rejoice that your names are written in heaven.

Rejoice insofar as you share Christ's sufferings, that you may also rejoice and be glad when his glory is revealed.

Rejoice and be glad, for your reward is great in heaven.

Rejoice in the Lord always; again I will say, Rejoice.

Clap your hands, all peoples!
  Shout to God with loud songs of joy!
For the LORD, the Most High, is to be feared,
  a great king over all the earth.

Be glad and rejoice,
  for the LORD has done great things!

Deut. 33:29; Is. 12:6; Deut. 26:11; Joel 2:23, 26; Rom. 12:12; Luke 10:20; 1 Pet. 4:13; Matt. 5:12; Phil. 4:4; Ps. 47:1-2; Joel 2:21 (All verses are from the ESV.)

Put Off the Old,
Put On the New

When you were pagans...you were influenced and led astray to mute idols.

You turned to God from idols to serve the living and true God, and to wait for his Son from heaven.

You were taught, with regard to your former way of life, to put off your old self, which is being corrupted by its deceitful desires; to be made new in the attitude of your minds; and to put on the new self, created to be like God in true righteousness and holiness.

For you have spent enough time in the past doing what pagans choose to do—living in debauchery, lust, drunkenness, orgies, carousing and detestable idolatry. They are surprised that you do not join them in their reckless, wild living, and they heap abuse on you. But they will have to give account to him who is ready to judge the living and the dead.

Get rid of the foreign gods you have with you, and purify yourselves and change your clothes.

Now you must also rid yourselves of all such things as these: anger, rage, malice, slander, and filthy language from your lips.

Rid yourselves of...all deceit, hypocrisy, envy.

Rather, clothe yourselves with the Lord Jesus Christ, and do not think about how to gratify the desires of the flesh.

As God's chosen people, holy and dearly loved, clothe yourselves with compassion, kindness, humility, gentleness and patience....And over all these virtues put on love, which binds them all together in perfect unity.

The night is nearly over; the day is almost here. So let us put aside the deeds of darkness and put on the armor of light.

1 Cor. 12:2; 1 Thess. 1:9-10; Eph. 4:22-24; 1 Pet. 4:3-5; Gen. 35:2; Col. 3:8; 1 Pet. 2:1; Rom. 13:14; Col. 3:12, 14; Rom. 13:12 (All verses are from the NIV.)

GOD AND JESUS SPEAK:

My Covenant

This is my covenant....My Spirit that is upon you, and my words that I have put in your mouth, shall not depart out of your mouth, or out of the mouth of your offspring, or out of the mouth of your children's offspring, from this time forth and forevermore.

I will never leave you nor forsake you.

I will never break my covenant with you.

For the mountains may depart
    and the hills be removed,
but my steadfast love shall not depart from you,
    and my covenant of peace shall not be removed.

Heaven and earth will pass away, but my words will not pass away.

I the LORD do not change; therefore you, O children of Jacob, are not consumed.

Whoever comes to me I will never cast out.

I will make with them an everlasting covenant, that I will not turn away from doing good to them. And I will put the fear of me in their hearts, that they may not turn from me.

For this is the covenant that I will make with the house of Israel...I will put my law within them, and I will write it on their hearts. And I will be their God, and they shall be my people. And no longer shall each one teach his neighbor and each his brother, saying, "Know the Lord," for they shall all know me, from the least of them to the greatest. For I will forgive their iniquity, and I will remember their sin no more.

For this is my blood of the covenant, which is poured out for many for the forgiveness of sins.

Is. 59:21; Heb. 13:5; Judg. 2:1; Is. 54:10; Matt. 24:35; Mal. 3:6; John 6:37; Jer. 32:40; Jer. 31:33-34; Matt. 26:28 (All verses are from the ESV.)

Care for Believers Worldwide

Love the brotherhood.

The gospel that has come to you...is bearing fruit and growing all over the world, just as it has among you.

For the promise is for you and for your children, and for all who are far off, as many as the Lord our God will call.

Pray at all times in the Spirit...with all perseverance and intercession for all the saints,

all those in every place who call on the name of Jesus Christ our Lord—both their Lord and ours,

all who have undying love for our Lord Jesus Christ.

For we were all baptized by one Spirit into one body....God has put the body together...so that...the members would have the same concern for each other. So if one member suffers, all the members suffer with it.

The same sufferings are being experienced by your fellow believers throughout the world.

Remember the prisoners, as though you were in prison with them, and the mistreated, as though you yourselves were suffering bodily.

Share with the saints in their needs.

We have heard of your faith in Christ Jesus and of the love you have for all the saints because of the hope reserved for you in heaven.

God is not unjust; He will not forget your work and the love you showed for His name when you served the saints—and you continue to serve them.

You are showing faithfulness by whatever you do for the brothers, especially when they are strangers.

1 Pet. 2:17; Col. 1:5-6; Acts 2:39; Eph. 6:18; 1 Cor. 1:2; Eph. 6:24; 1 Cor. 12:13, 24-26; 1 Pet. 5:9; Heb. 13:3; Rom. 12:13; Col. 1:4-5; Heb. 6:10; 3 John 1:5 (All verses are from the HCSB.)

The LORD Lightens My Darkness

The enemy has pursued my soul;
    he has crushed my life to the ground;
he has made me sit in darkness like those long dead.
    Therefore my spirit faints within me;
my heart within me is appalled.

I cry aloud to God,
    aloud to God, and he will hear me.
In the day of my trouble I seek the Lord;
    in the night my hand is stretched out without wearying.

For...the LORD my God lightens my darkness.

God my Maker...
    gives songs in the night.

God is light, and in him is no darkness at all.

God...has been my shepherd all my life long to this day.

God watched over me...
    His lamp shone upon my head,
and by his light I walked through darkness.

The light shines in the darkness, and the darkness has not overcome it.

The LORD is my light and my salvation;
    whom shall I fear?
The LORD is the stronghold of my life;
    of whom shall I be afraid?

Rejoice not over me, O my enemy;
    when I fall, I shall rise;
when I sit in darkness,
    the LORD will be a light to me.

Ps. 143:3-4; Ps. 77:1-2; Ps. 18:28; Job 35:10; 1 John 1:5; Gen. 48:15; Job 29:2-3; John 1:5; Ps. 27:1; Mic. 7:8 (All verses are from the ESV.)

I Will

O LORD, you are my God;
  I will exalt you.

I will trust in you.

I will be glad and exult in you.

I will delight in your statutes.

I will meditate on your precepts.

I will run in the way of your commandments.

I will sing praises to you.

I will tell of your name to my brothers.

I will teach transgressors your ways.

I will declare your greatness.

I will recount all of your wonderful deeds.

I will make known your faithfulness to all generations.

I will give thanks to you.

I will bless you as long as I live.

I will rejoice and be glad in your steadfast love.

I will glorify your name forever.

Is. 25:1; Ps. 55:23; Ps. 9:2; Ps. 119:16; Ps. 119:78; Ps. 119:32; Ps. 71:22; Ps. 22:22; Ps. 51:13; Ps. 145:6; Ps. 9:1; Ps. 89:1; Ps. 30:12; Ps. 63:4; Ps. 31:7; Ps. 86:12 (All verses are from the ESV.)

God Will Answer Our Prayers

We know that God does not listen to sinners, but if anyone is a worshiper of God and does his will, God listens to him.

The LORD is far from the wicked,
  but he hears the prayer of the righteous.

This is the confidence that we have toward him, that if we ask anything according to his will he hears us.

We do not know what to pray for as we ought, but the Spirit himself intercedes for us with groanings too deep for words.

And whatever we ask we receive from [God], because we keep his commandments and do what pleases him.

The LORD is near to all who call on him,
  to all who call on him in truth.
He fulfills the desire of those who fear him.

He who did not spare his own Son but gave him up for us all, how will he not also with him graciously give us all things?

[He] is able to do far more abundantly than all that we ask or think, according to the power at work within us.

Let us...with confidence draw near to the throne of grace, that we may receive mercy and find grace to help in time of need.

Let us draw near with a true heart in full assurance of faith.

God, our God, shall bless us.

John 9:31; Prov. 15:29; 1 John 5:14; Rom. 8:26; 1 John 3:22; Ps. 145:18-19; Rom. 8:32; Eph. 3:20; Heb. 4:16; Heb. 10:22; Ps. 67:6 (All verses are from the ESV.)

Better

It is better to be godly and have little
  than to be evil and rich.

Better to have little, with fear for the LORD,
  than to have great treasure and inner turmoil.

Better to be poor and honest
  than to be dishonest and a fool.

Better to live humbly with the poor
  than to share plunder with the proud.

Better a dry crust eaten in peace
  than a house filled with feasting—and conflict.

Better to spend your time at funerals than at parties.
  After all, everyone dies—
so the living should take this to heart.
  Sorrow is better than laughter,
for sadness has a refining influence on us.
  A wise person thinks a lot about death,
while a fool thinks only about having a good time.

Wisdom is better than strength.

Physical training is good, but training for godliness is much better, promising
benefits in this life and in the life to come.

How much better to get wisdom than gold,
  and good judgment than silver!

Choose a good reputation over great riches;
  being held in high esteem is better than silver or gold.

Ps. 37:16; Prov. 15:16; Prov. 19:1; Prov. 16:19; Prov. 17:1; Eccl. 7:2-4; Eccl. 9:16; 1 Tim. 4:8;
Prov. 16:16; Prov. 22:1 (All verses are from the NLT.)

We Proclaim Christ as Lord

We...have believed in Christ Jesus, in order to be justified by faith in Christ.

We make it our aim to please him,

our only Master and Lord, Jesus Christ.

For we must all appear before the judgment seat of Christ, so that each one may receive what is due for what he has done in the body, whether good or evil. Therefore, knowing the fear of the Lord, we persuade others.

We preach Christ crucified, a stumbling block to Jews and folly to Gentiles, but to those who are called, both Jews and Greeks, Christ the power of God and the wisdom of God.

The love of Christ controls us....He died for all, that those who live might no longer live for themselves but for him.

What we proclaim is not ourselves, but Jesus Christ as Lord.

Since we have the same spirit of faith according to what has been written, "I believed, and so I spoke," we also believe, and so we also speak, knowing that he who raised the Lord Jesus will raise us also with Jesus.

Whether we live or whether we die, we are the Lord's.

Since we have such a hope, we are very bold.

We are ambassadors for Christ, God making his appeal through us.

Thanks be to God, who...through us spreads the fragrance of the knowledge of him everywhere. For we are the aroma of Christ to God among those who are being saved and among those who are perishing, to one a fragrance from death to death, to the other a fragrance from life to life.

Gal. 2:16; 2 Cor. 5:9; Jude 1:4; 2 Cor. 5:10-11; 1 Cor. 1:23-24; 2 Cor. 5:14-15; 2 Cor. 4:5; 2 Cor. 4:13-14; Rom. 14:8; 2 Cor. 3:12; 2 Cor. 5:20; 2 Cor. 2:14-16 (All verses are from the ESV.)

GOD SPEAKS:

I Will Lead You

I am the LORD your God,
  who teaches you for your own good,
who leads you in the way you should go.

Walk only in the way that I command you, so that it may be well with you.

Do not turn from it to the right hand or to the left, so that you may be successful wherever you go.

Know that I am with you and will keep you wherever you go.

I will take you, one from a city and two from a family,
  and I will bring you to Zion.

I myself will be the shepherd of my sheep.

I will let them walk by brooks of water,
  in a straight path in which they shall not stumble.

I will bring them out from the peoples and gather them from the countries, and will bring them into their own land.

I will lead the blind
  by a road they do not know,
by paths they have not known
  I will guide them.
I will turn the darkness before them into light,
  the rough places into level ground.

I will turn all my mountains into a road,
  and my highways shall be raised up.

These are the things I will do,
  and I will not forsake them.

Is. 48:17; Jer. 7:23; Josh. 1:7; Gen. 28:15; Jer. 3:14; Ezek. 34:15; Jer. 31:9; Ezek. 34:13; Is. 42:16; Is. 49:11; Is. 42:16 (All verses are from the NRSV.)

The Lord's Garden

Shower, O heavens, from above,
  and let the skies rain down righteousness;
let the earth open, that salvation may spring up,
  and let it cause righteousness to sprout up also.

For as the earth brings forth its shoots,
  and as a garden causes what is sown in it to spring up,
so the Lord God will cause righteousness and praise
  to spring up before all the nations.

And they will say, "This land that was desolate has become like the garden of Eden."

For there shall be a sowing of peace; the vine shall yield its fruit, the ground
shall give its produce, and the skies shall give their dew.

Steadfast love and faithfulness will meet;
  righteousness and peace will kiss each other.
Faithfulness will spring up from the ground,
  and righteousness will look down from the sky.
The Lord will give what is good,
  and our land will yield its increase.
Righteousness will go before him,
  and will make a path for his steps.

Sow for yourselves righteousness;
  reap steadfast love;
break up your fallow ground;
  for it is time to seek the Lord,
that he may come and rain righteousness upon you.

Is. 45:8; Is. 61:11; Ezek. 36:35; Zech. 8:12; Ps. 85:10-13; Hos. 10:12 (All verses are from the NRSV.)

Blessed Is the Man

The LORD is good!
　　Blessed is the man who takes refuge in him!

Blessed is the man who makes
　　the LORD his trust,
who does not turn to the proud,
　　to those who go astray after a lie!

Blessed is the man
　　who walks not in the counsel of the wicked,
nor stands in the way of sinners,
　　nor sits in the seat of scoffers;
but his delight is in the law of the LORD,
　　and on his law he meditates day and night.

Blessed is the man who trusts in the LORD...
　　He is like a tree planted by water,
that sends out its roots by the stream,
　　and does not fear when heat comes,
for its leaves remain green,
　　and is not anxious in the year of drought,
for it does not cease to bear fruit.

Blessed is the man who fears the LORD...
　　His righteousness endures forever...
For the righteous will never be moved;
　　he will be remembered forever.
He is not afraid of bad news;
　　his heart is firm, trusting in the LORD.
His heart is steady; he will not be afraid,
　　until he looks in triumph on his adversaries.

Blessed is the man who remains steadfast under trial, for when he has stood the test
he will receive the crown of life, which God has promised to those who love him.

Ps. 34:8; Ps. 40:4; Ps. 1:1-2; Jer. 17:7-8; Ps. 112:1, 3, 6-8; James 1:12 (All verses are from the
ESV.)

Give Praise to God

Shout for joy to God, all the earth;
   sing the glory of his name;
give to him glorious praise!
   Say to God, "How awesome are your deeds!"

How manifold are your works!

Great is your power!

Strong is your hand!

How precious is your steadfast love, O God!

How abundant is your goodness!

Great is your faithfulness!

Great is your mercy!

How precious...are your thoughts, O God!

How sweet are your words!

True and just are your judgments!

Just and true are your ways!

O Lord, our Lord,
   how majestic is your name in all the earth!

Ps. 66:1-3; Ps. 104:24; Ps. 66:3; Ps. 89:13; Ps. 36:7; Ps. 31:19; Lam. 3:23; Ps. 119:156; Ps. 139:17; Ps. 119:103; Rev. 16:7; Rev. 15:3; Ps. 8:1 (All verses are from the ESV

From Death to Life

We know that we have passed from death to life.

You were dead in your transgressions and sins, in which you used to live when you followed the ways of this world and of the ruler of the kingdom of the air, the spirit who is now at work in those who are disobedient.

All of us also lived among them at one time, gratifying the cravings of our flesh and following its desires and thoughts. Like the rest, we were by nature deserving of wrath.

But because of his great love for us, God, who is rich in mercy, made us alive with Christ even when we were dead in transgressions.

The law of the Spirit who gives life has set you free from the law of sin and death.

Sin entered the world through one man, and death through sin, and in this way death came to all people, because all sinned.

But the Spirit gives life.

Inwardly we are being renewed day by day.

[God] has given us his very great and precious promises, so that through them you may participate in the divine nature, having escaped the corruption in the world caused by evil desires.

Do not offer any part of yourself to sin as an instrument of wickedness, but rather offer yourselves to God as those who have been brought from death to life—

> eternal life to which you were called,

> life that is truly life,

> life that is in Christ Jesus.

1 John 3:14; Eph. 2:1-2; Eph. 2:3; Eph. 2:4-5; Rom. 8:2; Rom. 5:12; 2 Cor. 3:6; 2 Cor. 4:16; 2 Pet. 1:4; Rom. 6:13; 1 Tim. 6:12; 1 Tim. 6:19; 2 Tim. 1:1 (All verses are from the NIV.)

He Cares for You

The Lord knows those who are his.

Anyone who loves God is known by him.

God knows your hearts.

Even the hairs of your head are all counted.

Your Father knows what you need before you ask him.

The LORD watches over the way of the righteous.

The eyes of the LORD are on the righteous,
   and his ears are open to their cry.

For the eyes of the LORD range throughout the entire earth, to strengthen those whose heart is true to him.

The LORD lifts up those who are bowed down;
   the LORD loves the righteous.

As the heavens are high above the earth,
   so great is his steadfast love toward those who fear him.

The LORD your God is God, the faithful God who maintains covenant loyalty with those who love him and keep his commandments.

The Father himself loves you.

Cast all your anxiety on him, because he cares for you.

2 Tim. 2:19; 1 Cor. 8:3; Luke 16:15; Luke 12:7; Matt. 6:8; Ps. 1:6; Ps. 34:15; 2 Chr. 16:9; Ps. 146:8; Ps. 103:11; Deut. 7:9; John 16:27; 1 Pet. 5:7 (All verses are from the NRSV.)

Do Not Love the World

You are not of the world.

You are but aliens and sojourners.

Do not love the world nor the things in the world. If anyone loves the world, the love of the Father is not in him. For all that is in the world, the lust of the flesh and the lust of the eyes and the boastful pride of life, is not from the Father, but is from the world.

Do you not know that friendship with the world is hostility toward God?

Many...are enemies of the cross of Christ, whose end is destruction, whose god is their appetite, and whose glory is in their shame, who set their minds on earthly things.

If you have been raised up with Christ, keep seeking the things above, where Christ is, seated at the right hand of God. Set your mind on the things above, not on the things that are on earth. For you have died and your life is hidden with Christ in God.

Therefore consider the members of your earthly body as dead to immorality, impurity, passion, evil desire, and greed, which amounts to idolatry. For it is because of these things that the wrath of God will come.

I urge you as aliens and strangers to abstain from fleshly lusts which wage war against the soul.

Do not be conformed to this world, but be transformed by the renewing of your mind, so that you may prove what the will of God is, that which is good and acceptable and perfect.

The world is passing away, and also its lusts; but the one who does the will of God lives forever.

John 15:19; Lev. 25:23; 1 John 2:15-16; James 4:4; Phil. 3:18-19; Col. 3:1-3; Col. 3:5-6; 1 Pet. 2:11; Rom. 12:2; 1 John 2:17 (All verses are from the NASB.)

JESUS SPEAKS:

The Cost of Being My Disciple

Whoever does not bear his own cross and come after me cannot be my disciple.

For which of you, desiring to build a tower, does not first sit down and count the cost, whether he has enough to complete it? Otherwise, when he has laid a foundation and is not able to finish, all who see it begin to mock him, saying, "This man began to build and was not able to finish."

So therefore, any one of you who does not renounce all that he has cannot be my disciple.

The kingdom of heaven is like treasure hidden in a field, which a man found and covered up. Then in his joy he goes and sells all that he has and buys that field.

Again, the kingdom of heaven is like a merchant in search of fine pearls, who, on finding one pearl of great value, went and sold all that he had and bought it.

If anyone comes to me and does not hate his own father and mother and wife and children and brothers and sisters, yes, and even his own life, he cannot be my disciple.

If anyone would come after me, let him deny himself and take up his cross daily and follow me. For whoever would save his life will lose it, but whoever loses his life for my sake will save it.

And everyone who has left houses or brothers or sisters or father or mother or children or lands, for my name's sake, will receive a hundredfold and will inherit eternal life.

Luke 14:27; Luke 14:28-30; Luke 14:33; Matt. 13:44; Matt. 13:45-46; Luke 14:26; Luke 9:23-24; Matt. 19:29 (All verses are from the ESV.)

Be Wise, My Son

Listen, my son. Accept my words....
   I am teaching you the way of wisdom...
Hold on to instruction; don't let go.
   Guard it, for it is your life.

Wisdom is supreme—so get wisdom.
   And whatever else you get, get understanding.

My son, if sinners entice you,
   don't be persuaded...
Don't travel that road with them.

Don't associate with those who drink too much wine
   or with those who gorge themselves on meat.

My son...though the lips of the forbidden woman drip honey
   and her words are smoother than oil,
in the end she's as bitter as wormwood
   and as sharp as a double-edged sword.
Her feet go down to death.

My son, pay attention to my words...
   Guard your heart above all else,
for it is the source of life.
   Don't let your mouth speak dishonestly,
and don't let your lips talk deviously.

My son, if your heart is wise,
   my heart will indeed rejoice.

My son, don't forget my teaching...
   Never let loyalty and faithfulness leave you.
Tie them around your neck;
   write them on the tablet of your heart.
Then you will find favor and high regard
   in the sight of God and man.

Prov. 4:10-11, 13; Prov. 4:7; Prov. 1:10, 15; Prov. 23:20; Prov. 5:1, 3-5; Prov. 4:20, 23-24; Prov. 23:15; Prov. 3:1, 3-4 (All verses are from the HCSB.)

God Is Sovereign

The earth is the LORD's, and everything in it,
the world, and all who live in it.

The LORD does whatever pleases him,
in the heavens and on the earth,
in the seas and all their depths.

[He] works out everything in conformity with the purpose of his will.

The LORD brings death and makes alive;
he brings down to the grave and raises up.
The LORD sends poverty and wealth;
he humbles and he exalts.

The Most High God is sovereign over all kingdoms on earth and sets over them
anyone he wishes.

He deposes kings and raises up others.

He brings princes to naught
and reduces the rulers of this world to nothing...
No sooner do they take root in the ground,
than he blows on them and they wither,
and a whirlwind sweeps them away like chaff.

He makes nations great, and destroys them;
he enlarges nations, and disperses them.

He does as he pleases
with the powers of heaven
and the peoples of the earth.
No one can hold back his hand.

The plans of the LORD stand firm forever,
the purposes of his heart through all generations.

Ps. 24:1; Ps. 135:6; Eph. 1:11; 1 Sam. 2:6-7; Dan. 5:21; Dan. 2:21; Is. 40:23-24; Job 12:23; Dan. 4:35;
Ps. 33:11 (All verses are from the NIV.)

Your Words Are the Delight of My Heart

You have the words of eternal life.

Your words were found, and I ate them,
   and your words became to me a joy
and the delight of my heart;
   for I am called by your name,
O LORD, God of hosts.

How sweet are your words to my taste,
   sweeter than honey to my mouth!

Your decrees are wonderful;
   therefore my soul keeps them.
The unfolding of your words gives light.

Your word is a lamp to my feet
   and a light to my path.

Your word is truth.

My heart stands in awe of your words.
   I rejoice at your word
like one who finds great spoil.

Oh, how I love your law!
   It is my meditation all day long.

My soul is consumed with longing
   for your ordinances at all times.

I will never forget your precepts,
   for by them you have given me life.

Your decrees are my heritage forever;
   they are the joy of my heart.

John 6:68; Jer. 15:16; Ps. 119:103; Ps. 119:129-130; Ps. 119:105; John 17:17; Ps. 119:161-162; Ps. 119:97; Ps. 119:20; Ps. 119:93; Ps. 119:111 (All verses are from the NRSV.)

Willing to Suffer
for Jesus

Prison and hardships are facing me. However, I consider my life worth nothing to me; my only aim is to finish the race and complete the task the Lord Jesus has given me—the task of testifying to the good news of God's grace.

I endure everything for the sake of the elect, that they too may obtain the salvation that is in Christ Jesus, with eternal glory.

I fill up in my flesh what is still lacking in regard to Christ's afflictions, for the sake of his body, which is the church.

Now I rejoice in what I am suffering.

And if I perish, I perish.

I am ready not only to be bound, but also to die...for the name of the Lord Jesus.

I want to know Christ—yes, to know the power of his resurrection and participation in his sufferings, becoming like him in his death, and so, somehow, attaining to the resurrection from the dead.

I eagerly expect and hope that I will in no way be ashamed, but will have sufficient courage so that now as always Christ will be exalted in my body, whether by life or by death. For to me, to live is Christ and to die is gain.

Do not be ashamed of the testimony about our Lord....Rather join with me in suffering for the gospel, by the power of God.

Acts 20:23-24; 2 Tim. 2:10; Col. 1:24; Col 1:24; Esth. 4:16; Acts 21:13; Phil. 3:10-11; Phil. 1:20-21; 2 Tim 1:8 (All verses are from the NIV.)

Be Unselfish

None of us lives to himself, and none of us dies to himself. For if we live, we live to the Lord, and if we die, we die to the Lord. So then, whether we live or whether we die, we are the Lord's.

Christ did not please himself, but as it is written, "The reproaches of those who reproached you fell on me."

For you know the grace of our Lord Jesus Christ, that though he was rich, yet for your sake he became poor, so that you by his poverty might become rich.

He died for all, that those who live might no longer live for themselves but for him.

Let no one seek his own good, but the good of his neighbor.

As each has received a gift, use it to serve one another, as good stewards of God's varied grace.

Wash one another's feet.

Do nothing from selfish ambition or conceit, but in humility count others more significant than yourselves.

Outdo one another in showing honor.

Love...does not insist on its own way.

Let each of you look not only to his own interests, but also to the interests of others.

Love one another with brotherly affection.

If you really fulfill the royal law according to the Scripture, "You shall love your neighbor as yourself," you are doing well.

Rom. 14:7-8; Rom. 15:3; 2 Cor. 8:9; 2 Cor. 5:15; 1 Cor. 10:24; 1 Pet. 4:10; John 13:14; Phil. 2:3; Rom. 12:10; 1 Cor. 13:4-5; Phil. 2:4; Rom. 12:10; James 2:8 (All verses are from the ESV.)

The Message of Salvation

God...commands all people everywhere to repent.

God does not show favoritism but accepts from every nation the one who fears him and does what is right.

For, "Everyone who calls on the name of the Lord will be saved." How, then, can they call on the one they have not believed in? And how can they believe in the one of whom they have not heard? And how can they hear without someone preaching to them? And how can anyone preach unless they are sent?

Faith comes from hearing the message, and the message is heard through the word about Christ.

God...gave us the ministry of reconciliation: that God was reconciling the world to himself in Christ, not counting people's sins against them. And he has committed to us the message of reconciliation,

the good news of peace through Jesus Christ, who is Lord of all.

The true message of the gospel...has come to you. In the same way, the gospel is bearing fruit and growing throughout the whole world—just as it has been doing among you since the day you heard it and truly understood God's grace.

Repentance for the forgiveness of sins will be preached in his name to all nations.

Those who were not told about him will see,
   and those who have not heard will understand.

Open your eyes and look at the fields! They are ripe for harvest.

The harvest is plentiful but the workers are few. Ask the Lord of the harvest, therefore, to send out workers into his harvest field.

Acts 17:30; Acts 10:34-35; Rom. 10:13-15; Rom. 10:17; 2 Cor. 5:18-19; Acts 10:36; Col. 1:5-6; Luke 24:47; Rom. 15:21; John 4:35; Matt. 9:37-38 (All verses are from the NIV.)

JESUS SPEAKS:

Come to Me

I have not come to call the righteous but sinners to repentance.

Whoever is of God hears the words of God.

My sheep hear my voice, and I know them, and they follow me.

No one can come to me unless it is granted him by the Father.

No one can come to me unless the Father who sent me draws him.

All that the Father gives me will come to me, and whoever comes to me I will never cast out.

Let the children come to me, and do not hinder them, for to such belongs the kingdom of God.

I have other sheep that are not of this fold. I must bring them also, and they will listen to my voice. So there will be one flock, one shepherd.

People will come from east and west, and from north and south, and recline at table in the kingdom of God.

Whoever comes to me shall not hunger, and whoever believes in me shall never thirst.

Come to me, all who labor and are heavy laden, and I will give you rest.

Come, you who are blessed by my Father.

Come, follow me.

Luke 5:32; John 8:47; John 10:27; John 6:65; John 6:44; John 6:37; Luke 18:16; John 10:16; Luke 13:29; John 6:35; Matt. 11:28; Matt. 25:34; Matt. 19:21 (All verses are from the ESV.)

Let Your Light Shine

Once you were full of darkness, but now you have light from the Lord.

You are all children of the light.

So live as people of light! For this light within you produces only what is good and right and true.

Carefully determine what pleases the Lord. Take no part in the worthless deeds of evil and darkness; instead, expose them.

Be...always ready to do what is good.

You are the light of the world—like a city on a hilltop that cannot be hidden. No one lights a lamp and then puts it under a basket. Instead, a lamp is placed on a stand, where it gives light to everyone in the house. In the same way, let your good deeds shine out for all to see, so that everyone will praise your heavenly Father.

Let your light shine for all to see.
  For the glory of the LORD rises to shine on you.

From...Zion, the perfection of beauty,
  God shines in glorious radiance.

Darkness as black as night covers all the nations of the earth,
  but the glory of the LORD rises and appears over you.
All nations will come to your light.

Always try to do good to each other and to all people.

Do everything without complaining and arguing, so that no one can criticize you. Live clean, innocent lives as children of God, shining like bright lights in a world full of crooked and perverse people.

Eph. 5:8; 1 Thess. 5:5; Eph. 5:8-9; Eph. 5:10-11; Titus 3:1; Matt. 5:14-16; Is. 60:1; Ps. 50:2; Is. 60:2-3; 1 Thess. 5:15; Phil. 2:14-15 (All verses are from the NLT.)

Do Not Envy

You are jealous of one another and quarrel with each other. Doesn't that prove you are controlled by your sinful nature? Aren't you living like people of the world?

But if you are bitterly jealous and there is selfish ambition in your heart, don't cover up the truth with boasting and lying. For jealousy and selfishness are not God's kind of wisdom. Such things are earthly, unspiritual, and demonic. For wherever there is jealousy and selfish ambition, there you will find disorder and evil of every kind.

Love is not jealous or boastful or proud.

Love each other deeply with all your heart. For you have been born again, but not to a life that will quickly end. Your new life will last forever because it comes from the eternal, living word of God. So get rid of all evil behavior. Be done with all deceit, hypocrisy, jealousy.

A peaceful heart leads to a healthy body;
    jealousy is like cancer in the bones.

Don't envy the wicked.
    For evil people have no future.

Don't...envy those who do wrong.
    For like grass, they soon fade away.
Like spring flowers, they soon wither.
    Trust in the LORD and do good.
Then you will live safely in the land and prosper.
    Take delight in the LORD,
and he will give you your heart's desires.

1 Cor. 3:3; James 3:14-16; 1 Cor. 13:4; 1 Pet. 1:22-23, 2:1; Prov. 14:30; Prov. 24:19-20; Ps. 37:1-4
(All verses are from the NLT.)

I Trust in You

I am trusting you, O LORD.

I look to you for help, O Sovereign LORD.
   You are my refuge.

You are my rock and my fortress.

I trust in your unfailing love.

I cling to you;
   your strong right hand holds me securely.

You, O LORD, are a shield around me.

You are my hiding place;
   you protect me from trouble.
You surround me with songs of victory.

When I am afraid,
   I will put my trust in you.

I know that you can do anything.

You will keep in perfect peace
   all who trust in you,
all whose thoughts are fixed on you!

In peace I will lie down and sleep,
   for you alone, O LORD, will keep me safe.

You guard all that is mine.

My future is in your hands.

O LORD, I give my life to you.
   I trust in you, my God!

Ps. 31:14; Ps. 141:8; Ps. 31:3; Ps. 13:5; Ps. 63:8; Ps. 3:3; Ps. 32:7; Ps. 56:3; Job 42:2; Is. 26:3; Ps. 4:8;
Ps. 16:5; Ps. 31:15; Ps. 25:1-2 (All verses are from the NLT.)

He Who Promised
Is Faithful

The Lord is faithful. He will establish you and guard you against the evil one.

I am sure of this, that he who began a good work in you will bring it to completion at the day of Jesus Christ.

God is not man, that he should lie,
  or a son of man, that he should change his mind.
Has he said, and will he not do it?
  Or has he spoken, and will he not fulfill it?

The grass withers, the flower fades,
  but the word of our God will stand forever.

Know...that the LORD your God is God, the faithful God who keeps covenant and steadfast love with those who love him and keep his commandments.

He has caused us to be born again to a living hope through the resurrection of Jesus Christ from the dead, to an inheritance that is imperishable, undefiled, and unfading, kept in heaven for you, who by God's power are being guarded through faith for a salvation ready to be revealed in the last time.

God...has also put his seal on us and given us his Spirit in our hearts as a guarantee.

Let us hold fast the confession of our hope without wavering, for he who promised is faithful.

And this is the promise that he made to us—eternal life,

eternal life, which God, who never lies, promised before the ages began.

Now may the God of peace himself sanctify you completely, and may your whole spirit and soul and body be kept blameless at the coming of our Lord Jesus Christ. He who calls you is faithful; he will surely do it.

2 Thess. 3:3; Phil. 1:6; Num. 23:19; Is. 40:8; Deut. 7:9; 1 Pet. 1:3-5; 2 Cor. 1:21-22; Heb. 10:23; 1 John 2:25; Titus 1:2; 1 Thess. 5:23-24 (All verses are from the ESV.)

Seek

Seek the LORD, all you humble of the land,
  who do his just commands.

Seek the LORD and his strength;
  seek his presence continually!

Seek his kingdom.

Seek righteousness.

Seek humility.

Seek peace and pursue it.

Pursue...godliness, faith, love, steadfastness, gentleness.

Seek out all the commandments of the LORD your God.

Seek good, and not evil,
  that you may live.

Seek the things that are above.

Seek the city that is to come.

To those who by patience in well-doing seek for glory and honor and
immortality, [God] will give eternal life.

Blessed are those who keep his testimonies,
  who seek him with their whole heart.

Set your mind and heart to seek the LORD your God.

Zeph. 2:3; 1 Chr. 16:11; Luke 12:31; Zeph. 2:3; Zeph. 2:3; 1 Pet. 3:11; 1 Tim. 6:11; 1 Chr. 28:8;
Amos 5:14; Col. 3:1; Heb. 13:14; Rom. 2:7; Ps. 119:2; 1 Chr. 22:19 (All verses are from the ESV.)

God's Love for Us

In this the love of God was made manifest among us, that God sent his only Son into the world, so that we might live through him.

When the goodness and loving kindness of God our Savior appeared, he saved us, not because of works done by us in righteousness, but according to his own mercy.

God shows his love for us in that while we were still sinners, Christ died for us.

See what kind of love the Father has given to us, that we should be called children of God; and so we are.

So we have come to know and to believe the love that God has for us.

I will recount the steadfast love of the LORD,

> who establishes us...in Christ,

> who daily bears us up,

> who comforts us in all our affliction,

> who richly provides us with everything to enjoy,

> who gives us the victory through our Lord Jesus Christ.

I am sure that neither death nor life, nor angels nor rulers, nor things present nor things to come, nor powers, nor height nor depth, nor anything else in all creation, will be able to separate us from the love of God in Christ Jesus our Lord.

1 John 4:9; Titus 3:4-5; Rom. 5:8; 1 John 3:1; 1 John 4:16; Is. 63:7; 2 Cor. 1:21; Ps. 68:19; 2 Cor. 1:4; 1 Tim. 6:17; 1 Cor. 15:57; Rom. 8:38-39 (All verses are from the ESV.)

GOD SPEAKS:
I Am

I am God, and there is no other;
  I am God, and there is no one like Me.

I am who I am.

I, the LORD, am the maker of all things.

I am God Almighty.

I am the LORD your God, who brought you out of the...house of slavery.

I, the LORD, am your Savior
  and your Redeemer.

I, the LORD, am your healer.

I am a master to you.

I am a shield to you.

I am your portion and your inheritance.

I am the LORD, your Holy One.

I am a great King, and My name is feared among the nations.

I am the Alpha and the Omega, the beginning and the end.

I am the first and I am the last,
  and there is no God besides Me.

Is. 46:9; Ex. 3:14; Is. 44:24; Gen. 17:1; Ex. 20:2; Is. 60:16; Ex. 15:26; Jer. 3:14; Gen. 15:1; Num. 18:20; Is. 43:15; Mal. 1:14; Rev. 21:6; Is. 44:6 (All verses are from the NASB.)

Put Your Hope in the LORD

Put your hope in the LORD.
   For there is faithful love with the LORD,
and with Him is redemption in abundance.

You who believe in the name of the Son of God...may know that you have eternal life.

The promise is for you and for your children, and for all who are far off, as many as the Lord our God will call.

Rejoice in hope; be patient in affliction.

Light shines in the darkness for the upright.

The darkness is passing away and the true light is already shining,

the light of life.

[Jesus] is the beginning,
   the firstborn from the dead.

He who raised Christ from the dead will also bring your mortal bodies to life through His Spirit who lives in you.

The world with its lust is passing away, but the one who does God's will remains forever.

Always fear the LORD.
   For then you will have a future,
and your hope will never fade.

Put your hope in the LORD,
   both now and forever.

May the God of hope fill you with all joy and peace as you believe in Him so that you may overflow with hope by the power of the Holy Spirit.

Ps. 130:7; 1 John 5:13; Acts 2:39; Rom. 12:12; Ps. 112:4; 1 John 2:8; John 8:12; Col. 1:18; Rom. 8:11; 1 John 2:17; Prov. 23:17-18; Ps. 131:3; Rom. 15:13 (All verses are from the HCSB.)

The LORD Will Take Vengeance

The LORD is a jealous and avenging God...
   The LORD takes vengeance on his foes
and vents his wrath against his enemies.
   The LORD is slow to anger but great in power;
the LORD will not leave the guilty unpunished.

Will not God bring about justice for his chosen ones, who cry out to him day and night? Will he keep putting them off? I tell you, he will see that they get justice, and quickly.

For he who avenges blood remembers;
   he does not ignore the cries of the afflicted.

See, the LORD is coming out of his dwelling
   to punish the people of the earth for their sins.
The earth will disclose the blood shed on it;
   the earth will conceal its slain no longer.

God is just: He will pay back trouble to those who trouble you.

For whoever touches you touches the apple of his eye.

Bless those who persecute you; bless and do not curse....Do not take revenge, my dear friends, but leave room for God's wrath, for it is written: "It is mine to avenge; I will repay," says the Lord.

On the contrary:
   "If your enemy is hungry, feed him;
      if he is thirsty, give him something to drink.
   In doing this, you will heap burning coals on his head."
Do not be overcome by evil, but overcome evil with good.

Do not repay evil with evil or insult with insult. On the contrary, repay evil with blessing, because to this you were called so that you may inherit a blessing.

Nah. 1:2-3; Luke 18:7-8; Ps. 9:12; Is. 26:21; 2 Thess. 1:6; Zech. 2:8; Rom. 12:14, 19; Rom. 12:20-21; 1 Pet. 3:9 (All verses are from the NIV.)

A Prayer for God's People

Blessed are the people who know the festal shout,
who walk, O LORD, in the light of your face,
who exult in your name all the day
and in your righteousness are exalted.
For you are the glory of their strength.

Oh, how abundant is your goodness,
which you have stored up for those who fear you...
In the cover of your presence you hide them
from the plots of men;
you store them in your shelter
from the strife of tongues.

May they be secure who love you!

Spread your protection over them,
that those who love your name may exult in you.

Keep them in your name...that they may be one.

Peace and mercy be upon them.

Let your work be shown to your servants,
and your glorious power to their children.

Direct their hearts toward you.

May all who seek you
rejoice and be glad in you!
May those who love your salvation
say evermore, "God is great!"

Let them ever sing for joy.

Oh, save your people and bless your heritage!
Be their shepherd and carry them forever.

Ps. 89:15-17; Ps. 31:19-20; Ps. 122:6; Ps. 5:11; John 17:11; Gal. 6:16; Ps. 90:16; 1 Chr. 29:18;
Ps. 70:4; Ps. 5:11; Ps. 28:9 (All verses are from the ESV.)

Jesus Is...

Jesus is the Son of God,

    the Beloved,

    the radiance of the glory of God,

    the exact imprint of his nature.

He is the propitiation for our sins,

    the Righteous One,

    the Lamb of God,

    the Savior of the world.

He is the mediator of a new covenant,

    the founder and perfecter of our faith,

    the head of the church,

    the great shepherd of the sheep.

He is the beginning, the firstborn from the dead,

    the heir of all things,

    the King.

He is the true God and eternal life,

    the living one,

    the Amen.

1 John 5:5; Eph. 1:6; Heb. 1:3; Heb. 1:3; 1 John 2:2; Acts 22:14; John 1:29; 1 John 4:14; Heb. 9:15; Heb. 12:2; Eph. 5:23; Heb. 13:20; Col. 1:18; Heb. 1:2; Matt. 25:34; 1 John 5:20; Rev. 1:18; Rev. 3:14 (All verses are from the ESV.)

Prayers That Are Heard

Jesus told this parable: "Two men went up to the temple to pray, one a Pharisee and the other a tax collector. The Pharisee stood by himself and prayed: 'God, I thank you that I am not like other people—robbers, evildoers, adulterers—or even like this tax collector. I fast twice a week and give a tenth of all I get.' But the tax collector...would not even look up to heaven, but beat his breast and said, 'God, have mercy on me, a sinner.' I tell you that this man, rather than the other, went home justified before God."

God opposes the proud
  but shows favor to the humble.

When you pray, do not be like the hypocrites, for they love to pray standing in the synagogues and on the street corners to be seen by others. Truly I tell you, they have received their reward in full. But when you pray, go into your room, close the door and pray to your Father, who is unseen. Then your Father, who sees what is done in secret, will reward you.

And when you pray, do not keep on babbling like pagans, for they think they will be heard because of their many words. Do not be like them, for your Father knows what you need before you ask him.

The eyes of the Lord are on the righteous
  and his ears are attentive to their prayer.

The prayer of a righteous person is powerful and effective. Elijah was a human being, even as we are. He prayed earnestly that it would not rain, and it did not rain on the land for three and a half years. Again he prayed, and the heavens gave rain, and the earth produced its crops.

The righteous cry out, and the LORD hears them;
  he delivers them from all their troubles.

Luke 18:9-14; James 4:6; Matt. 6:5-6; Matt. 6:7-8; 1 Pet. 3:12; James 5:16-18; Ps. 34:17 (All verses are from the NIV.)

As For Me...

The fool says in his heart,
  "There is no God."
They are corrupt, and their ways are vile;
  there is no one who does good.

But as for me and my household, we will serve the LORD.

What [the godless] trust in is fragile;
  what they rely on is a spider's web.
They lean on the web, but it gives way;
  they cling to it, but it does not hold.

As for me, I call to God,
  and the LORD saves me.

Those who are far from [God] will perish...
  But as for me, it is good to be near God.
I have made the Sovereign LORD my refuge.

Those who trust in idols,
  who say to images, "You are our gods,"
will be turned back in utter shame.

But as for me, I watch in hope for the LORD,
  I wait for God my Savior...
He will bring me out into the light;
  I will see his righteousness.

Ps. 53:1; Josh. 24:15; Job 8:14-15; Ps. 55:16; Ps. 73:27-28; Is. 42:17; Micah 7:7, 9 (All verses are from the NIV.)

JESUS SPEAKS:

Entering the Kingdom

Repent, for the kingdom of heaven has come near.

Not everyone who says to me, "Lord, Lord," will enter the kingdom of heaven, but only the one who does the will of my Father who is in heaven.

I tell you that unless your righteousness surpasses that of the Pharisees and the teachers of the law, you will certainly not enter the kingdom of heaven.

Make every effort to enter through the narrow door, because many, I tell you, will try to enter and will not be able to.

Enter through the narrow gate. For wide is the gate and broad is the road that leads to destruction, and many enter through it. But small is the gate and narrow the road that leads to life, and only a few find it.

If your eye causes you to stumble, pluck it out. It is better for you to enter the kingdom of God with one eye than to have two eyes and be thrown into hell, where
> "the worms that eat them do not die,
> and the fire is not quenched."

Truly I tell you, anyone who will not receive the kingdom of God like a little child will never enter it.

Truly I tell you, it is hard for someone who is rich to enter the kingdom of heaven. Again I tell you, it is easier for a camel to go through the eye of a needle than for someone who is rich to enter the kingdom of God....With man this is impossible, but with God all things are possible.

Very truly I tell you, no one can enter the kingdom of God unless they are born of water and the Spirit....You must be born again.

I am the gate; whoever enters through me will be saved.

Matt. 4:17; Matt. 7:21; Matt. 5:20; Luke 13:24; Matt. 7:13-14; Mark 9:47-48; Mark 10:15; Matt. 19:23-24, 26; John 3:5, 7; John 10:9 (All verses are from the NIV.)

Our Future Glory

In his kindness God called you to share in his eternal glory by means of Christ Jesus.

For God knew his people in advance, and he chose them to become like his Son, so that his Son would be the firstborn among many brothers and sisters. And having chosen them, he called them to come to him. And having called them, he gave them right standing with himself. And having given them right standing, he gave them his glory.

Together with Christ we are heirs of God's glory. But if we are to share his glory, we must also share his suffering.

Yet what we suffer now is nothing compared to the glory he will reveal to us later. For all creation is waiting eagerly for that future day when God will reveal who his children really are.

[We] can see and reflect the glory of the Lord. And the Lord—who is the Spirit—makes us more and more like him as we are changed into his glorious image.

We never give up. Though our bodies are dying, our spirits are being renewed every day. For our present troubles are small and won't last very long. Yet they produce for us a glory that vastly outweighs them and will last forever!

When Christ, who is your life, is revealed to the whole world, you will share in all his glory.

When the Great Shepherd appears, you will receive a crown of never-ending glory and honor.

1 Pet. 5:10; Rom. 8:29-30; Rom. 8:17; Rom. 8:18-19; 2 Cor. 3:18; 2 Cor. 4:16-17; Col. 3:4; 1 Pet. 5:4 (All verses are from the NLT.)

New Life: Raised, Reborn, Re-created

God, being rich in mercy, because of the great love with which he loved us, even when we were dead in our trespasses, made us alive together with Christ.

We have passed out of death into life.

We were buried...with [Christ] by baptism into death, in order that, just as Christ was raised from the dead by the glory of the Father, we too might walk in newness of life,

raised with him through faith in the powerful working of God.

According to his great mercy, [God] has caused us to be born again.

Of his own will he brought us forth by the word of truth.

Everyone who believes that Jesus is the Christ has been born of God,

born, not of blood nor of the will of the flesh nor of the will of man, but of God.

If anyone is in Christ, he is a new creation. The old has passed away; behold, the new has come,

the new self, which is being renewed in knowledge after the image of its creator.

We are his workmanship, created in Christ Jesus for good works,

created after the likeness of God in true righteousness and holiness.

Eph. 2:4-5; 1 John 3:14; Rom. 6:4; Col. 2:12; 1 Pet. 1:3; James 1:18; 1 John 5:1; John 1:13; 2 Cor. 5:17; Col. 3:10; Eph. 2:10; Eph. 4:24 (All verses are from the ESV.)

Your Name

Father, hallowed be your name.

You are great, and your name is great in might.

Your name, O LORD, endures forever,
  your renown, O LORD, throughout all ages.

I will glorify your name forever.

Turn to me and be gracious to me,
  as is your custom toward those who love your name.

For your name's sake, O LORD,
  pardon my guilt.

For your name's sake, O LORD, preserve my life.

For your name's sake lead me and guide me.

Give me an undivided heart to revere your name.

Remember this, O LORD, how the enemy scoffs,
  and an impious people reviles your name...
Do not let the downtrodden be put to shame;
  let the poor and needy praise your name.
Rise up, O God, plead your cause.

Act, O LORD, for your name's sake.

All the nations you have made shall come
  and bow down before you, O Lord,
and shall glorify your name.

Your name will be magnified forever.

Luke 11:2; Jer. 10:6; Ps. 135:13; Ps. 86:12; Ps. 119:132; Ps. 25:11; Ps. 143:11; Ps. 31:3; Ps. 86:11; Ps. 74:18, 21-22; Jer. 14:7; Ps. 86:9; 2 Sam. 7:26 (All verses are from the NRSV.)

The Blood of Jesus

The law of Moses was only a shadow, a dim preview of the good things to come, not the good things themselves. The sacrifices under that system were repeated again and again, year after year, but they were never able to provide perfect cleansing for those who came to worship.

For it is not possible for the blood of bulls and goats to take away sins.

Under the old covenant, the priest stands and ministers before the altar day after day, offering the same sacrifices again and again, which can never take away sins. But our High Priest offered himself to God as a single sacrifice for sins, good for all time.

Christ has now become the High Priest over all the good things that have come. He has entered that greater, more perfect Tabernacle in heaven, which was not made by human hands and is not part of this created world. With his own blood—not the blood of goats and calves—he entered the Most Holy Place once for all time and secured our redemption forever.

By that one offering he forever made perfect those who are being made holy.

We have been made right in God's sight by the blood of Christ,

the blood of the covenant, which made us holy.

The blood of Jesus...cleanses us from all sin.

[God] is so rich in kindness and grace that he purchased our freedom.

The ransom he paid was not mere gold or silver. It was the precious blood of Christ, the sinless, spotless Lamb of God.

Heb. 10:1; Heb. 10:4; Heb. 10:11-12; Heb. 9:11-12; Heb. 10:14; Rom. 5:9; Heb. 10:29; 1 John 1:7; Eph. 1:7; 1 Pet. 1:18-19 (All verses are from the NLT.)

Final Destinies

My feet had almost slipped;
  I had nearly lost my foothold.
For I envied the arrogant
  when I saw the prosperity of the wicked.
They have no struggles;
  their bodies are healthy and strong.
They are free from common human burdens;
  they are not plagued by human ills...
When I tried to understand all this,
  it troubled me deeply
till I entered the sanctuary of God;
  then I understood their final destiny.

Their destiny is destruction, their god is their stomach, and their glory is in their shame.

For the wages of sin is death, but the gift of God is eternal life in Christ Jesus our Lord.

You who believe in the name of the Son of God...may know that you have eternal life.

Do not let your heart envy sinners,
  but always be zealous for the fear of the LORD.

Be still before the LORD
  and wait patiently for him;
do not fret when people succeed in their ways,
  when they carry out their wicked schemes.
Refrain from anger and turn from wrath;
  do not fret—it leads only to evil.
For those who are evil will be destroyed.

They will go away to eternal punishment, but the righteous to eternal life.

Ps. 73:2-5, 16-17; Phil. 3:19; Rom. 6:23; 1 John 5:13; Prov. 23:17; Ps. 37:7-9; Matt. 25:46 (All verses are from the NIV.)

There Is a God in Heaven

There is a God in heaven

>who is high and lifted up,

>who is righteous and mighty,

>who is great and awesome,

>who is worthy to be praised,

>who alone does great wonders,

>who gives life to all things,

>who justifies the ungodly,

>who raises the dead,

>who practices steadfast love, justice, and righteousness,

>who works all things according to the counsel of his will,

>who inhabits eternity,

>who is and who was and who is to come.

The LORD lives!

The LORD, he is God.

Let all the earth fear the LORD;
>let all the inhabitants of the world stand in awe of him!

Dan. 2:28; Is. 57:15; Job 34:17; Neh. 4:14; 2 Sam. 22:4; Ps. 136:4; 1 Tim. 6:13; Rom. 4:5; 2 Cor. 1:9; Jer. 9:24; Eph. 1:11; Is. 57:15; Rev. 1:8; Ps. 18:46; 1 Kin. 18:39; Ps. 33:8 (All verses are from the ESV.)

JESUS SPEAKS:

Words of Comfort

Do not let your hearts be troubled. Believe in God, believe also in me.

The Lord...has anointed me
  to bring good news to the poor.
He has sent me to proclaim release to the captives
  and recovery of sight to the blind,
to let the oppressed go free.

Come to me, all you that are weary and are carrying heavy burdens, and I will give you rest. Take my yoke upon you, and learn from me; for I am gentle and humble in heart, and you will find rest for your souls. For my yoke is easy, and my burden is light.

Do not worry, saying, "What will we eat?" or "What will we drink?" or "What will we wear?"

You are worried and distracted by many things; there is need of only one thing.

Strive first for the kingdom of God and his righteousness, and all these things will be given to you as well.

Are not five sparrows sold for two pennies? Yet not one of them is forgotten in God's sight. But even the hairs of your head are all counted. Do not be afraid; you are of more value than many sparrows.

In me you may have peace. In the world you face persecution. But take courage; I have conquered the world!

I will ask the Father, and he will give you another Advocate, to be with you forever. This is the Spirit of truth, whom the world cannot receive, because it neither sees him nor knows him. You know him, because he abides with you, and he will be in you.

Peace I leave with you; my peace I give to you. I do not give to you as the world gives. Do not let your hearts be troubled, and do not let them be afraid.

John 14:1; Luke 4:18-19; Matt. 11:28-30; Matt. 6:31; Luke 10:41-42; Matt. 6:33; Luke 12:6-7; John 16:33; John 14:16-17; John 14:27 (All verses are from the NRSV.)

The Creator of This World

In the beginning was the Word, and the Word was with God, and the Word was God. He was in the beginning with God. All things came into being through Him, and apart from Him nothing came into being that has come into being.

In the beginning God created the heavens and the earth.

By the word of God the heavens existed long ago and the earth was formed out of water and by water.

The earth was formless and void, and darkness was over the surface of the deep, and the Spirit of God was moving over the surface of the waters. Then God said, "Let there be light"; and there was light.

In six days the Lord made the heavens and the earth, the sea and all that is in them, and rested on the seventh day; therefore the Lord blessed the sabbath day and made it holy.

God saw all that He had made, and behold, it was very good.

Great are the works of the LORD;
  they are studied by all who delight in them.

Remember...your Creator in the days of your youth, before the evil days come.

For the wrath of God is revealed from heaven against all ungodliness and unrighteousness of men who suppress the truth in unrighteousness, because that which is known about God is evident within them; for God made it evident to them. For since the creation of the world His invisible attributes, His eternal power and divine nature, have been clearly seen, being understood through what has been made, so that they are without excuse.

They exchanged the truth of God for a lie, and worshiped and served the creature rather than the Creator, who is blessed forever. Amen.

John 1:1-3; Gen. 1:1; 2 Pet. 3:5; Gen. 1:2-3; Ex. 20:11; Gen. 1:31; Ps. 111:2; Eccl. 12:1; Rom. 1:18-20; Rom. 1:25 (All verses are from the NASB.)

The Testing of Your Faith

The crucible is for silver, and the furnace is for gold,
and the LORD tests hearts.

Beloved, do not be surprised at the fiery trial when it comes upon you to test
you, as though something strange were happening to you.

You have been grieved by various trials, so that the tested genuineness of your
faith—more precious than gold that perishes though it is tested by fire—may be
found to result in praise and glory and honor at the revelation of Jesus Christ.

Count it all joy, my brothers, when you meet trials of various kinds, for you
know that the testing of your faith produces steadfastness. And let steadfastness
have its full effect, that you may be perfect and complete, lacking in nothing.

Blessed is the man who remains steadfast under trial, for when he has stood the test
he will receive the crown of life, which God has promised to those who love him.

He has fixed a day on which he will judge the world in righteousness.

Each one's work will become manifest, for the Day will disclose it, because it will
be revealed by fire, and the fire will test what sort of work each one has done.

Therefore do not pronounce judgment before the time, before the Lord comes,
who will bring to light the things now hidden in darkness and will disclose the
purposes of the heart. Then each one will receive his commendation from God.

Prov. 17:3; 1 Pet. 4:12; 1 Pet. 1:6-7; James 1:2-4; James 1:12; Acts 17:31; 1 Cor. 3:13; 1 Cor. 4:5
(All verses are from the ESV.)

Blessed Be the LORD

Bless the LORD, O my soul,
  and all that is within me,
bless his holy name.

Blessed be the LORD,
  for he has wondrously shown his steadfast love to me.

Blessed be the LORD, my rock.

The LORD gave, and the LORD has taken away; blessed be the name of the LORD.

Bless the LORD, O my soul.
  O LORD my God, you are very great.

Blessed be your glorious name, which is exalted above all blessing and praise....
You are the LORD, you alone; you have made heaven, the heaven of heavens,
with all their host, the earth and all that is on it, the seas and all that is in them.
To all of them you give life, and the host of heaven worships you.

All your works shall give thanks to you, O LORD,
  and all your faithful shall bless you.
They shall speak of the glory of your kingdom,
  and tell of your power,
to make known to all people your mighty deeds,
  and the glorious splendor of your kingdom.

I will extol you, my God and King,
  and bless your name forever and ever.
Every day I will bless you,
  and praise your name forever and ever.

Ps. 103:1; Ps. 31:21; Ps. 144:1; Job 1:21; Ps. 104:1; Neh. 9:5-6; Ps. 145:10-12; Ps. 145:1-2 (All verses are from the NRSV.)

A Missionary's
Prayer Requests

It has always been my ambition to preach the gospel where Christ was not known, so that...

"Those who were not told about him will see,
and those who have not heard will understand."

I urge you, brothers and sisters, by our Lord Jesus Christ and by the love of the Spirit, to join me in my struggle by praying to God for me.

Pray...that whenever I speak, words may be given me so that I will fearlessly make known the mystery of the gospel,

that I may proclaim it clearly, as I should.

And pray for us, too, that God may open a door for our message.

Pray for us that the message of the Lord may spread rapidly and be honored,

so that the grace that is reaching more and more people may cause thanksgiving to overflow to the glory of God.

Pray that we may be delivered from wicked and evil people, for not everyone has faith.

Pray...that I may come to you with joy, by God's will, and in your company be refreshed.

You help us by your prayers. Then many will give thanks on our behalf for the gracious favor granted us in answer to the prayers of many.

Rom.15:20-21; Rom. 15:30; Eph. 6:19; Col. 4:4; Col. 4:3; 2 Thess. 3:1; 2 Cor. 4:15; 2 Thess. 3:2; Rom. 15:31-32; 2 Cor.1:11 (All verses are from the NIV.)

Help the Poor

Give justice to the poor and the orphan;
  uphold the rights of the oppressed and the destitute.
Rescue the poor and helpless;
  deliver them from the grasp of evil people.

Those who oppress the poor insult their Maker,
  but helping the poor honors him.

Pure and genuine religion in the sight of God the Father means caring for
orphans and widows in their distress and refusing to let the world corrupt you.

Sodom's sins were pride, gluttony, and laziness, while the poor and needy
suffered outside her door.

Sell your possessions and give to those in need. This will store up treasure for
you in heaven! And the purses of heaven never get old or develop holes. Your
treasure will be safe; no thief can steal it and no moth can destroy it.

When you put on a luncheon or a banquet...invite the poor, the crippled, the
lame, and the blind. Then at the resurrection of the righteous, God will reward
you for inviting those who could not repay you.

If you help the poor, you are lending to the LORD—
  and he will repay you!

Oh, the joys of those who are kind to the poor!
  The LORD rescues them when they are in trouble.
The LORD protects them
  and keeps them alive.
He gives them prosperity in the land
  and rescues them from their enemies.

Blessed are those who help the poor.

Ps. 82:3-4; Prov. 14:31; James 1:27; Ezek. 16:49; Luke 12:33; Luke 14:12-14; Prov. 19:17; Ps. 41:1-2;
Prov. 14:21 (All verses are from the NLT.)

The LORD's Discipline

Do not despise the LORD's instruction, my son,
    and do not loathe His discipline;
for the LORD disciplines the one He loves,
    just as a father, the son he delights in.

We had natural fathers discipline us, and we respected them. Shouldn't we submit even more to the Father of spirits and live? For they disciplined us for a short time based on what seemed good to them, but He does it for our benefit, so that we can share His holiness.

When we are judged, we are disciplined by the Lord, so that we may not be condemned with the world.

God certainly does all these things...to a man
    in order to turn him back from the Pit,
so he may shine with the light of life.

Should we accept only good from God and not adversity?

No discipline seems enjoyable at the time, but painful. Later on, however, it yields the fruit of peace and righteousness to those who have been trained by it.

We know that all things work together for the good of those who love God.

See how happy the man is God corrects;
    so do not reject the discipline of the Almighty.
For He crushes but also binds up;
    He strikes, but His hands also heal.

Humble yourselves...under the mighty hand of God, so that He may exalt you at the proper time.

Prov. 3:11-12; Heb. 12:9-10; 1 Cor. 11:32; Job 33:29-30; Job 2:10; Heb. 12:11; Rom. 8:28; Job 5:17-18; 1 Pet. 5:6 (All verses are from the HCSB.)

GOD SPEAKS:

God Describes Himself

I the LORD your God am holy.

You cannot see my face, for man shall not see me and live.

To whom will you liken me and make me equal,
 and compare me, that we may be alike?

Only in the LORD, it shall be said of me,
 are righteousness and strength.

My thoughts are not your thoughts,
 neither are your ways my ways,
For as the heavens are higher than the earth,
 so are my ways higher than your ways
and my thoughts than your thoughts.

I the LORD speak the truth;
 I declare what is right.

I live forever.

I the LORD do not change; therefore you, O children of Jacob, are not consumed.

I am compassionate.

The LORD, the LORD, a God merciful and gracious, slow to anger, and abounding in steadfast love and faithfulness, keeping steadfast love for thousands, forgiving iniquity and transgression and sin, but who will by no means clear the guilty.

I am the LORD who practices steadfast love, justice, and righteousness in the earth. For in these things I delight.

Lev. 19:2; Ex. 33:20; Is. 46:5; Is. 45:24; Is. 55:8-9; Is. 45:19; Deut. 32:40; Mal. 3:6; Ex. 22:27; Ex. 34:6-7; Jer. 9:24 (All verses are from the ESV.)

Spiritual Blindness

Unless one is born again he cannot see the kingdom of God.

The natural person does not accept the things of the Spirit of God, for they are folly to him, and he is not able to understand them because they are spiritually discerned.

The word of the cross is folly to those who are perishing.

Whoever does evil has not seen God.

The way of the wicked is like deep darkness;
   they do not know over what they stumble.

Whoever hates his brother is in the darkness and walks in the darkness, and does not know where he is going, because the darkness has blinded his eyes.

The LORD opens the eyes of the blind.

The LORD...has made his light to shine upon us.

And we have seen his glory, glory as of the only Son from the Father, full of grace and truth.

The god of this world has blinded the minds of the unbelievers, to keep them from seeing the light of the gospel of the glory of Christ, who is the image of God.

The Lord said...."I am sending you to open their eyes, so that they may turn from darkness to light and from the power of Satan to God, that they may receive forgiveness of sins and a place among those who are sanctified by faith in me."

John 3:3; 1 Cor. 2:14; 1 Cor. 1:18; 3 John 1:11; Prov. 4:19; 1 John 2:11; Ps. 146:8; Ps. 118:27; John 1:14; 2 Cor. 4:4; Acts 26:15, 17-18 (All verses are from the ESV.)

God Has Given Us the Spirit

God...saved us...by the washing of regeneration and renewal of the Holy Spirit.

For in one Spirit we were all baptized.

God has sent the Spirit of his Son into our hearts, crying, "Abba! Father!"

The Spirit himself bears witness with our spirit that we are children of God.

God's love has been poured into our hearts through the Holy Spirit,

who is the guarantee of our inheritance until we acquire possession of it, to the praise of his glory.

Now we have received not the spirit of the world, but the Spirit who is from God, that we might understand the things freely given us by God.

By this we know that we abide in him and he in us, because he has given us of his Spirit.

We...worship by the Spirit of God.

Likewise the Spirit helps us in our weakness. For we do not know what to pray for as we ought, but the Spirit himself intercedes for us with groanings too deep for words.

It is the Spirit who gives life.

If we live by the Spirit, let us also keep in step with the Spirit.

The fruit of the Spirit is love, joy, peace, patience, kindness, goodness, faithfulness, gentleness, self-control.

Titus 3:4-5; 1 Cor. 12:13; Gal. 4:6; Rom. 8:16; Rom. 5:5; Eph. 1:14; 1 Cor. 2:12; 1 John 4:13; Phil. 3:3; Rom. 8:26; John 6:63; Gal. 5:25; Gal. 5:22-23 (All verses are from the ESV.)

I Love You, O Lord

I love you, O Lord, my strength.

You, O Lord, are a God merciful and gracious,
   slow to anger and abounding in steadfast love and faithfulness.

You, O Lord, are good and forgiving.

You are righteous.

You are just.

I am yours.

I know that you delight in me.

I love your precepts.

I do your commandments.

I rejoice in your salvation.

I give you thanks, O Lord, with my whole heart.

I will sing praises to you,
   for you, O God, are my fortress,
the God who shows me steadfast love.

My soul clings to you.

Let me dwell in your tent forever!

Ps. 18:1; Ps. 86:15; Ps. 86:5; Neh. 9:8; Ezra 9:15; Ps. 119:94; Ps. 41:11; Ps. 119:159; Ps. 119:166; 1 Sam. 2:1; Ps. 138:1; Ps. 59:17; Ps. 63:8; Ps. 61:4 (All verses are from the ESV.)

Made Blameless in Christ

Do not be deceived: neither the sexually immoral, nor idolaters, nor adulterers, nor men who practice homosexuality, nor thieves, nor the greedy, nor drunkards, nor revilers, nor swindlers will inherit the kingdom of God. And such were some of you.

You, who once were alienated and hostile in mind, doing evil deeds, [Christ] has now reconciled in his body of flesh by his death, in order to present you holy and blameless and above reproach before him.

You are clean.

You were washed, you were sanctified, you were justified in the name of the Lord Jesus Christ and by the Spirit of our God.

Christ loved the church and gave himself up for her, that he might sanctify her, having cleansed her by the washing of water with the word, so that he might present the church to himself in splendor, without spot or wrinkle or any such thing, that she might be holy and without blemish.

For by a single offering he has perfected for all time those who are being sanctified.

[God] is able to...present you blameless before the presence of his glory with great joy.

Though your sins are like scarlet,
   they shall be as white as snow;
though they are red like crimson,
   they shall become like wool.

Now may the God of peace himself sanctify you completely, and may your whole spirit and soul and body be kept blameless at the coming of our Lord Jesus Christ.

1 Cor. 6:9-11; Col. 1:21-22; John 15:3; 1 Cor. 6:11; Eph. 5:25-27; Heb. 10:14; Jude 1:24; Is. 1:18; 1 Thess. 5:23 (All verses are from the ESV.)

Running for the Prize

I consider my life worth nothing to me; my only aim is to finish the race and complete the task the Lord Jesus has given me.

I do not run like someone running aimlessly.

One thing I do: Forgetting what is behind and straining toward what is ahead, I press on toward the goal to win the prize for which God has called me heavenward in Christ Jesus.

You were running a good race. Who cut in on you to keep you from obeying the truth? That kind of persuasion does not come from the one who calls you.

Do you not know that in a race all the runners run, but only one gets the prize? Run in such a way as to get the prize.

Let us throw off everything that hinders and the sin that so easily entangles. And let us run with perseverance the race marked out for us, fixing our eyes on Jesus, the pioneer and perfecter of faith. For the joy set before him he endured the cross, scorning its shame, and sat down at the right hand of the throne of God. Consider him who endured such opposition from sinners, so that you will not grow weary and lose heart.

Strengthen your feeble arms and weak knees. "Make level paths for your feet," so that the lame may not be disabled, but rather healed.

Everyone who competes in the games goes into strict training. They do it to get a crown that will not last, but we do it to get a crown that will last forever.

I have fought the good fight, I have finished the race, I have kept the faith. Now there is in store for me the crown of righteousness, which the Lord, the righteous Judge, will award to me on that day.

Acts 20:24; 1 Cor. 9:26; Phil. 3:13-14; Gal. 5:7-8; 1 Cor. 9:24; Heb. 12:1-3; Heb. 12:12-13; 1 Cor. 9:25; 2 Tim. 4:7-8 (All verses are from the NIV.)

Wait for the LORD

The LORD...will rise up to show mercy to you.
  For the LORD is a God of justice;
blessed are all those who wait for him.

The LORD is good to those who wait for him,
  to the soul that seeks him.

Those who wait for the LORD shall renew their strength,
  they shall mount up with wings like eagles,
they shall run and not be weary,
  they shall walk and not faint.

Be still before the LORD, and wait patiently for him;
  do not fret over those who prosper in their way,
over those who carry out evil devices.
  Refrain from anger, and forsake wrath.
Do not fret—it leads only to evil.

It is good that one should wait quietly
  for the salvation of the LORD.

Wait for the LORD, and keep to his way,
  and he will exalt you to inherit the land;
you will look on the destruction of the wicked.

Be strong, and let your heart take courage;
  wait for the LORD!

Hold fast to love and justice,
  and wait continually for your God.

Is. 30:18; Lam. 3:25; Is. 40:31; Ps. 37:7-8; Lam. 3:26; Ps. 37:34; Ps. 27:14; Hos. 12:6 (All verses are from the NRSV.)

GOD AND JESUS SPEAK:

I Will Reward You

I...examine the mind,
   I test the heart
to give to each...according to what his actions deserve.

The cowards, unbelievers, vile, murderers, sexually immoral, sorcerers, idolaters, and all liars—their share will be in the lake that burns with fire and sulfur, which is the second death.

But the righteous one will live by his faith.

That slave whose master finds him working when he comes will be rewarded.

Then the King will say to those on His right, "Come...inherit the kingdom prepared for you from the foundation of the world.
   For I was hungry
      and you gave Me something to eat;
   I was thirsty
      and you gave Me something to drink;
   I was a stranger and you took Me in;
      I was naked and you clothed Me;
   I was sick and you took care of Me;
      I was in prison and you visited Me...
I assure you: Whatever you did for one of the least of these brothers of Mine, you did for Me."

Whoever gives just a cup of cold water to one of these little ones because he is a disciple—I assure you: He will never lose his reward!

Love your enemies, do what is good, and lend, expecting nothing in return. Then your reward will be great.

I know your works.

Look! I am coming quickly, and My reward is with Me to repay each person according to what he has done.

Jer. 17:10; Rev. 21:8; Hab. 2:4; Luke 12:43; Matt. 25:34-36, 40; Matt. 10:42; Luke 6:35; Rev. 3:8; Rev. 22:12 (All verses are from the HCSB.)

We Are the Body of Christ

The human body has many parts, but the many parts make up one whole body. So it is with the body of Christ....We have all been baptized into one body by one Spirit.

We are members of his body.

Just as our bodies have many parts and each part has a special function, so it is with Christ's body....In his grace, God has given us different gifts for doing certain things well.

If the whole body were an eye, how would you hear? Or if your whole body were an ear, how would you smell anything? But our bodies have many parts, and God has put each part just where he wants it.

The eye can never say to the hand, "I don't need you." The head can't say to the feet, "I don't need you." In fact, some parts of the body that seem weakest and least important are actually the most necessary.

We are many parts of one body, and we all belong to each other.

If one part suffers, all the parts suffer with it, and if one part is honored, all the parts are glad.

Christ...is the Savior of his body, the church.

No one hates his own body but feeds and cares for it, just as Christ cares for the church.

We will...[grow] in every way more and more like Christ, who is the head of his body, the church. He makes the whole body fit together perfectly. As each part does its own special work, it helps the other parts grow, so that the whole body is healthy and growing and full of love.

1 Cor. 12:12-13; Eph. 5:30; Rom. 12:4-6; 1 Cor. 12:17-18; 1 Cor. 12:21-22; Rom. 12:5; 1 Cor. 12:26; Eph. 5:23; Eph. 5:29; Eph. 4:15-16 (All verses are from the NLT.)

Praise the LORD

How great is the LORD,
  how deserving of praise.

Acknowledge that the LORD is God!
  He made us, and we are his.

Worship the LORD with gladness.
  Come before him, singing with joy.

Enter his gates with thanksgiving;
  go into his courts with praise.
Give thanks to him and praise his name.
  For the LORD is good.
His unfailing love continues forever,
  and his faithfulness continues to each generation.

Praise the Lord; praise God our savior!
  For each day he carries us in his arms.

Sing about the glory of his name!
  Tell the world how glorious he is.

Sing to him; yes, sing his praises.
  Tell everyone about his wonderful deeds.

Praise him for his mighty works;
  praise his unequaled greatness!

Sing to the LORD a new song.
  Sing his praises in the assembly of the faithful...
For the LORD delights in his people;
  he crowns the humble with victory.

Praise the LORD forever!
  Amen and amen!

Ps. 48:1; Ps. 100:3; Ps. 100:2; Ps. 100:4-5; Ps. 68:19; Ps. 66:2; Ps. 105:2; Ps. 150:2; Ps. 149:1, 4;
Ps. 89:52 (All verses are from the NLT.)

You Will Receive Me to Glory

The lines have fallen for me in pleasant places;
  indeed, I have a beautiful inheritance.

Surely goodness and mercy shall follow me
  all the days of my life,
and I shall dwell in the house of the LORD
  forever.

O Lord...you guide me with your counsel,
  and afterward you will receive me to glory.
Whom have I in heaven but you?
  And there is nothing on earth that I desire besides you.

My soul longs for your salvation;
  I hope in your word.
My eyes long for your promise.

My heart is glad, and my whole being rejoices;
  my flesh also dwells secure.
For you will not abandon my soul to Sheol,
  or let your holy one see corruption.

You...will revive me again;
  from the depths of the earth
you will bring me up again.

And in your steadfast love you will cut off my enemies,
  and you will destroy all the adversaries of my soul,
for I am your servant.

I shall behold your face in righteousness;
  when I awake, I shall be satisfied with your likeness.

You will make me full of gladness with your presence.

And I will glorify your name forever.

Ps. 16:6; Ps. 23:6; Ps. 73:20, 24-25; Ps. 119:81-82; Ps. 16:9-10; Ps. 71:20; Ps. 143:12; Ps. 17:15;
Acts 2:28; Ps. 86:12 (All verses are from the ESV.)

Jesus, Our High Priest

We have a great High Priest who has entered heaven, Jesus the Son of God.

Our High Priest offered himself to God as a single sacrifice for sins, good for all time. Then he sat down in the place of honor at God's right hand.

Christ did not enter into a holy place made with human hands, which was only a copy of the true one in heaven. He entered into heaven itself to appear now before God on our behalf.

We have an advocate who pleads our case before the Father. He is Jesus Christ, the one who is truly righteous.

For there is only one God and one Mediator who can reconcile God and humanity—the man Christ Jesus.

This High Priest of ours understands our weaknesses, for he faced all of the same testings we do, yet he did not sin.

He is the kind of high priest we need because he is holy and blameless, unstained by sin.

Because Jesus lives forever, his priesthood lasts forever. Therefore he is able, once and forever, to save those who come to God through him. He lives forever to intercede with God on their behalf.

Since we have a great High Priest who rules over God's house, let us go right into the presence of God with sincere hearts fully trusting him. For our guilty consciences have been sprinkled with Christ's blood to make us clean, and our bodies have been washed with pure water.

Heb. 4:14; Heb. 10:12; Heb. 9:24; 1 John 2:1; 1 Tim. 2:5; Heb. 4:15; Heb. 7:26; Heb. 7:24-25; Heb. 10:21-22 (All verses are from the NLT.)

Be Diligent

You shall diligently keep the commandments of the LORD your God.

You shall teach them diligently to your children, and shall talk of them when you sit in your house, and when you walk by the way, and when you lie down, and when you rise.

Diligently listen to the voice of the LORD your God, and do that which is right in his eyes.

Be diligent to be found by him without spot or blemish.

Make every effort to supplement your faith with virtue, and virtue with knowledge, and knowledge with self-control, and self-control with steadfastness, and steadfastness with godliness, and godliness with brotherly affection, and brotherly affection with love....Be all the more diligent to confirm your calling and election, for if you practice these qualities you will never fall.

Take care, and keep your soul diligently, lest you forget the things that your eyes have seen, and lest they depart from your heart all the days of your life.

Remain faithful to the Lord with steadfast purpose.

Be steadfast, immovable, always abounding in the work of the Lord, knowing that in the Lord your labor is not in vain.

Be...imitators of those who through faith and patience inherit the promises.

Deut. 6:17; Deut. 6:7; Ex. 15:26; 2 Pet. 3:14; 2 Pet. 1:5-7, 10; Deut. 4:9; Acts 11:23; 1 Cor. 15:58; Heb. 6:12 (All verses are from the ESV.)

The Good Person

The good person out of the good treasure of his heart produces good...for out of the abundance of the heart his mouth speaks.

The law of his God is in his heart.

The mouth of the righteous utters wisdom,
   and his tongue speaks justice.

He...does not slander with his tongue
   and does no evil to his neighbor,
nor takes up a reproach against his friend.

He...does not lift up his soul to what is false
   and does not swear deceitfully.

He is gracious, merciful, and righteous.

He...does not defile his neighbor's wife...does not oppress anyone, but restores to the debtor his pledge, commits no robbery, gives his bread to the hungry and covers the naked with a garment, does not lend at interest or take any profit, withholds his hand from injustice, executes true justice between man and man.

He who does these things shall never be moved.

His soul shall abide in well-being.

A good man will be filled with the fruit of his ways.

He will receive blessing from the LORD
   and righteousness from the God of his salvation.

Luke 6:45; Ps. 37:31; Ps. 37:30; Ps. 15:2-3; Ps. 24:4; Ps. 112:4; Ezek. 18:6-8; Ps. 15:5; Ps. 25:13; Prov. 14:14; Ps. 24:5 (All verses are from the ESV.)

JESUS SPEAKS:

Promises for the Righteous

Blessed...are those who hear the word of God and obey it!

For the hour is coming when all who are in their graves will...come out—those who have done good, to the resurrection of life.

They will inherit the earth.

They will be comforted.

They will be filled.

They will receive mercy.

They will see God.

They will be called children of God.

Theirs is the kingdom of heaven.

The righteous will shine like the sun in the kingdom of their Father.

They will walk with me, dressed in white, for they are worthy.

And they will never perish.

Luke 11:28; John 5:28-29; Matt. 5:5; Matt. 5:4; Matt. 5:6; Matt. 5:7; Matt. 5:8; Matt. 5:9; Matt. 5:3; Matt. 13:43; Rev. 3:4; John 10:28 (All verses are from the NRSV.)

We Will Serve the LORD

We are the servants of the God of heaven and earth.

He is our God.

We are his people.

Great is our Lord.

Great is his steadfast love toward us.

The LORD has done great things for us.

He has caused us to be born again.

We are God's children now.

We must obey God rather than men.

We will serve the LORD.

All that the LORD has spoken we will do.

God gave us eternal life, and this life is in his Son.

We will walk in the name of the LORD our God
　　forever and ever.

We will bless the LORD
　　from this time forth and forevermore.

Ezra 5:11; Josh. 24:18; Ps. 100:3; Ps. 147:5; Ps. 117:2; Ps. 126:3; 1 Pet. 1:3; 1 John 3:2; Acts 5:29; Josh. 24:15; Ex. 19:8; 1 John 5:11; Mic. 4:5; Ps. 115:18 (All verses are from the ESV.)

The Source of My Strength

The LORD is my strength and my shield;
  in him my heart trusts;
so I am helped, and my heart exults,
  and with my song I give thanks to him.

GOD, the Lord, is my strength;
  he makes my feet like the feet of a deer,
and makes me tread upon the heights.

I am filled with power,
  with the spirit of the LORD.

I can do all things through him who strengthens me.

He makes me lie down in green pastures;
  he leads me beside still waters;
he restores my soul.

I toil and struggle with all the energy that [Christ] powerfully inspires within me.

He said to me, "My grace is sufficient for you, for power is made perfect in weakness." So, I will boast all the more gladly of my weaknesses, so that the power of Christ may dwell in me. Therefore I am content with weaknesses, insults, hardships, persecutions, and calamities for the sake of Christ; for whenever I am weak, then I am strong.

My flesh and my heart may fail,
  but God is the strength of my heart
and my portion forever.

Ps. 28:7; Hab. 3:19; Mic. 3:8; Phil. 4:13; Ps. 23:2-3; Col. 1:29; 2 Cor. 12:9-10; Ps. 73:26 (All verses are from the NRSV.)

Your Creation

O LORD...I ponder all your great works
and think about what you have done.

Long ago you laid the foundation of the earth
and made the heavens with your hands.

You made the starlight and the sun.
You set the boundaries of the earth,
and you made both summer and winter.

When I look at the night sky and see the work of your fingers—
the moon and the stars you set in place—
what are mere mortals that you should think about them,
human beings that you should care for them?

O LORD, what a variety of things you have made!
In wisdom you have made them all.
The earth is full of your creatures.
Here is the ocean, vast and wide,
teeming with life of every kind,
both large and small...
They all depend on you
to give them food as they need it.

You alone are the LORD. You made the skies and the heavens and all the stars.
You made the earth and the seas and everything in them. You preserve them all.

You are worthy, O Lord...
to receive glory and honor and power.
For you created all things,
and they exist because you created what you pleased.

Ps. 143:1, 5; Ps. 102:25; Ps. 74:16-17; Ps. 8:3-4; Ps. 104:24-25, 27; Neh. 9:6; Rev. 4:11 (All verses
are from the NLT.)

Blessed Are Those
Who Fear the LORD

Blessed are all who fear the LORD,
who walk in obedience to him.

The LORD confides in those who fear him;
he makes his covenant known to them.

The eyes of the LORD are on those who fear him,
on those whose hope is in his unfailing love.

He fulfills the desires of those who fear him;
he hears their cry and saves them.

The angel of the LORD encamps around those who fear him,
and he delivers them.

For as high as the heavens are above the earth,
so great is his love for those who fear him.

As a father has compassion on his children,
so the LORD has compassion on those who fear him.

His mercy extends to those who fear him,
from generation to generation.

He provides food for those who fear him;
he remembers his covenant forever.

Fear the LORD, you his holy people,
for those who fear him lack nothing.

Ps. 128:1; Ps. 25:14; Ps. 33:18; Ps. 145:19; Ps. 34:7; Ps. 103:11; Ps. 103:13; Luke 1:50; Ps. 111:5; Ps. 34:9 (All verses are from the NIV.)

Questions from Job, Answers from Jesus

Where shall wisdom be found?

I am the way, and the truth, and the life.

Learn from me.

Who can bring a clean thing out of an unclean?

My blood...is poured out for many for the forgiveness of sins.

Be clean.

How can a man be in the right before God?

Everyone who acknowledges me before men, I also will acknowledge before my Father who is in heaven.

And he who loves me will be loved by my Father.

Does not [God] see my ways
and number all my steps?

Why, even the hairs of your head are all numbered. Fear not.

If a man dies, shall he live again?

I am the resurrection and the life. Whoever believes in me, though he dies, yet shall he live.

What is my strength, that I should wait?
And what is my end, that I should be patient?

I will come again and will take you to myself.

Be faithful unto death, and I will give you the crown of life.

Job 28:12; John 14:6; Matt. 11:29; Job 14:4; Matt. 26:28; Luke 5:13; Job 9:2; Matt. 10:32; John 14:21; Job 31:4; Luke 12:7; Job 14:14; John 11:25; Job 6:11; John 14:3; Rev. 2:10 (All verses are from the ESV.)

The LORD Is Our King

The LORD is our king.

The LORD has established his throne in the heavens,
  and his kingdom rules over all.

The LORD reigns; he is robed in majesty.

Righteousness and justice are the foundation of his throne.

Come, let us worship and bow down;
  let us kneel before the LORD.

He is the King of glory,

Lord of heaven and earth,

the blessed and only Sovereign, the King of kings and Lord of lords, who alone
has immortality, who dwells in unapproachable light, whom no one has ever
seen or can see. To him be honor and eternal dominion.

All the ends of the earth shall remember
    and turn to the LORD,
and all the families of the nations
    shall worship [him].
For kingship belongs to the LORD,
    and he rules over the nations...
Before him shall bow all who go down to the dust.

The LORD will reign forever and ever.

His kingdom shall never be destroyed.

With trumpets and the sound of the horn
  make a joyful noise before the King, the LORD!

To the King of the ages, immortal, invisible, the only God, be honor and glory
forever and ever. Amen.

Is. 33:22; Ps. 103:19; Ps. 93:1; Ps. 97:2; Ps. 95:6; Ps. 24:10; Luke 10:21; 1 Tim. 6:15-16; Ps. 22:27-
29; Ex. 15:18; Dan. 6:26; Ps. 98:6; 1 Tim. 1:17 (All verses are from the ESV.)

JESUS SPEAKS:

Giving

It is more blessed to give than to receive.

Give to him who asks of you, and do not turn away from him who wants to borrow from you.

Give, and it will be given to you. They will pour into your lap a good measure—pressed down, shaken together, and running over. For by your standard of measure it will be measured to you in return.

Beware of practicing your righteousness before men to be noticed by them; otherwise you have no reward with your Father who is in heaven. So when you give to the poor, do not sound a trumpet before you, as the hypocrites do in the synagogues and in the streets, so that they may be honored by men. Truly I say to you, they have their reward in full.

But when you give to the poor, do not let your left hand know what your right hand is doing, so that your giving will be in secret; and your Father who sees what is done in secret will reward you.

When you give a reception, invite the poor, the crippled, the lame, the blind, and you will be blessed, since they do not have the means to repay you; for you will be repaid at the resurrection of the righteous.

If you lend to those from whom you expect to receive, what credit is that to you? Even sinners lend to sinners in order to receive back the same amount. But love your enemies, and do good, and lend, expecting nothing in return; and your reward will be great, and you will be sons of the Most High; for He Himself is kind to ungrateful and evil men. Be merciful, just as your Father is merciful.

Sell your possessions and give to charity; make yourselves money belts which do not wear out, an unfailing treasure in heaven, where no thief comes near nor moth destroys. For where your treasure is, there your heart will be also.

Acts 20:35; Matt. 5:42; Luke 6:38; Matt. 6:1-2; Matt. 6:3-4; Luke 14:13-14; Luke 6:34-36; Luke 12:33-34 (All verses are from the NASB.)

God Is Able to Deliver Us

The Lord knows how to rescue the godly from trials.

The Lord drove the [Red] sea back by a strong east wind all night and made the sea dry land, and the waters were divided. And the people of Israel went into the midst of the sea on dry ground, the waters being a wall to them on their right hand and on their left.

The waters returned and covered the chariots and the horsemen; of all the host of Pharaoh that had followed them into the sea, not one of them remained.... Thus the Lord saved Israel that day from the hand of the Egyptians.

Shadrach, Meshach, and Abednego...were thrown into the burning fiery furnace.

God...sent his angel and delivered his servants, who trusted in him.

The fire had [no] power over the bodies of those men. The hair of their heads was not singed, their cloaks were not harmed, and no smell of fire had come upon them.

Daniel was brought and cast into the den of lions....God sent his angel and shut the lions' mouths....Daniel was taken up out of the den, and no kind of harm was found on him, because he had trusted in his God.

Behold, these are but the outskirts of his ways,
   and how small a whisper do we hear of him!
But the thunder of his power who can understand?

He who has saved Daniel
   from the power of the lions

is able to do far more abundantly than all that we ask or think.

Our God whom we serve is able to deliver us.

2 Pet. 2:9; Ex. 14:21-22; Ex. 14:28, 30; Dan. 3:20-21; Dan. 3:28; Dan. 3:27; Dan. 6:16, 22-23; Job 26:14; Dan. 6:27; Eph. 3:20; Dan. 3:17 (All verses are from the ESV.)

Jesus' Glory

Because of the joy awaiting him, [Jesus] endured the cross, disregarding its shame.

He humbled himself in obedience to God
  and died a criminal's death on a cross.
Therefore, God elevated him to the place of highest honor
  and gave him the name above all other names,
that at the name of Jesus every knee should bow,
  in heaven and on earth and under the earth.

Jesus...was given a position "a little lower than the angels"; and because he suffered death for us, he is now "crowned with glory and honor."

God put him in the place of honor at his right hand as Prince and Savior.

Now he is far above any ruler or authority or power or leader or anything else—not only in this world but also in the world to come. God has put all things under the authority of Christ.

God promised everything to the Son as an inheritance.

We are God's children....Together with Christ we are heirs of God's glory. But if we are to share his glory, we must also share his suffering.

When the Son of Man comes in his glory, and all the angels with him, then he will sit upon his glorious throne.

And he will reign forever and ever.

Worthy is the Lamb who was slaughtered—
  to receive power and riches
and wisdom and strength
  and honor and glory and blessing.

Heb. 12:2; Phil. 2:8-10; Heb. 2:9; Acts 5:31; Eph. 1:21-22; Heb. 1:2; Rom. 8:16-17; Matt. 25:31; Rev. 11:15; Rev. 5:12 (All verses are from the NLT.)

A Prayer for Wisdom

Teach me how to live, O LORD.
　Lead me along the right path.

You made me; you created me.
　Now give me the sense to follow your commands.

Give me...wisdom and knowledge.

Open my eyes to see
　the wonderful truths in your instructions.

Look upon me with love;
　teach me your decrees.

Teach me good judgment.

Give me an understanding heart so that I can...know the difference between
right and wrong.

I have tried hard to find you—
　don't let me wander from your commands.

Don't let me drift toward evil
　or take part in acts of wickedness.

Turn my eyes from worthless things,
　and give me life through your word.

Joyful are those you discipline, LORD,
　those you teach with your instructions.

Give me understanding and I will obey your instructions;
　I will put them into practice with all my heart.

Ps. 27:11; Ps. 119:73; 2 Chr. 1:10; Ps. 119:18; Ps. 119:135; Ps. 119:66; 1 Kin. 3:9; Ps. 119:10;
Ps. 141:4; Ps. 119:37; Ps. 94:12; Ps. 119:34 (All verses are from the NLT.)

God Will Be With You
in the Wilderness

The LORD watches over the way of the righteous.

In a desert land he found [Jacob],
   in a barren and howling waste.
He shielded him and cared for him;
   he guarded him as the apple of his eye...
The LORD alone led him.

[God's people] did not thirst when he led them through the deserts;
   he made water flow for them from the rock.

The LORD your God has blessed you in all the work of your hands. He has watched over your journey through this vast wilderness....The LORD your God has been with you, and you have not lacked anything.

The LORD will guide you always.

Although the Lord gives you the bread of adversity and the water of affliction... your ears will hear a voice behind you, saying, "This is the way; walk in it."

He will sustain you.

He will satisfy your needs in a sun-scorched land
   and will strengthen your frame.
You will be like a well-watered garden,
   like a spring whose waters never fail.

The LORD watches over you—
   the LORD is your shade at your right hand;
the sun will not harm you by day,
   nor the moon by night.

Do not be afraid...for the LORD your God goes with you

through the valley of the shadow of death.

Ps. 1:6; Deut. 32:10-12; Is. 48:21; Deut. 2:7; Is. 58:11; Is. 30:20-21; Ps. 55:22; Is. 58:11; Ps. 121:5-6; Deut. 31:6; Ps. 23:4 (All verses are from the NIV.)

Obey the LORD's Commandments

What does the LORD your God require of you, but to fear the LORD your God, to walk in all his ways, to love him, to serve the LORD your God with all your heart and with all your soul, and to keep the commandments and statutes of the LORD?

Has the LORD as great delight in burnt offerings and sacrifices,
   as in obeying the voice of the LORD?
Behold, to obey is better than sacrifice,
   and to listen than the fat of rams.

And his commandments are not burdensome.

This commandment...is not too hard for you, neither is it far off...But the word is very near you. It is in your mouth and in your heart, so that you can do it.

This is love, that we walk according to his commandments.

You shall not turn aside to the right hand or to the left. You shall walk in all the way that the LORD your God has commanded you, that you may live, and that it may go well with you, and that you may live long in the land that you shall possess.

Whoever does the will of God abides forever.

Whoever keeps his commandments abides in God, and God in him.

Fear the LORD and serve him faithfully with all your heart. For consider what great things he has done for you.

The steadfast love of the LORD is from everlasting to everlasting
   on those who fear him,
and his righteousness to children's children,
   to those who keep his covenant
and remember to do his commandments.

Deut 10:12-13; 1 Sam. 15:22; 1 John 5:3; Deut. 30:11, 14; 2 John 1:6; Deut. 5:32-33; 1 John 2:17; 1 John 3:24; 1 Sam. 12:24; Ps. 103:17-18 (All verses are from the ESV.)

Sayings of the Proud

Who is the LORD, that I should obey his voice?

I will not listen.

It is vain to serve God.

It profits a man nothing
    that he should take delight in God.

There is no God.

He did not make me.

By the strength of my hand I have [succeeded],
    and by my wisdom, for I have understanding.

My power and the might of my hand have gotten me this wealth.

I am rich, I have prospered, and I need nothing.

I have not sinned.

I am not unclean.

Where is your God?

Where is the promise of his coming?

Who will bring me down to the ground?

I shall not be moved.

I shall be safe, though I walk in the stubbornness of my heart.

Ex. 5:2; Jer. 22:21; Mal. 3:14; Job 34:9; Ps. 53:1; Is. 29:16; Is. 10:13; Deut. 8:17; Rev. 3:17; Jer. 2:35; Jer. 2:23; Ps. 42:3; 2 Pet. 3:4; Obad. 1:3; Ps. 10:6; Deut. 29:19 (All verses are from the ESV.)

GOD AND JESUS SPEAK:
Humble Yourself

Let not the wise man boast in his wisdom, let not the mighty man boast in his might, let not the rich man boast in his riches, but let him who boasts boast in this, that he understands and knows me.

This is the one to whom I will look:
   he who is humble and contrite in spirit
and trembles at my word.

Blessed are the poor in spirit, for theirs is the kingdom of heaven.

Whoever humbles himself like [a] child is the greatest in the kingdom of heaven.

Truly, I say to you, unless you turn and become like children, you will never enter the kingdom of heaven.

At the set time that I appoint
   I will judge with equity...
I say to the boastful, "Do not boast."

I will punish the world for its evil,
   and the wicked for their iniquity;
I will put an end to the pomp of the arrogant,
   and lay low the pompous pride of the ruthless.

But whoever would be great among you must be your servant, and whoever would be first among you must be your slave, even as the Son of Man came not to be served but to serve.

Everyone who exalts himself will be humbled, but the one who humbles himself will be exalted.

Jer. 9:23-24; Is. 66:2; Matt. 5:3; Matt. 18:4; Matt. 18:3; Ps. 75:2, 4; Is. 13:11; Matt. 20:26-28; Luke 18:14 (All verses are from the ESV.)

Sayings of the Humble

O Lord, my heart is not lifted up,
 my eyes are not raised too high;
I do not occupy myself with things
 too great and too marvelous for me.

You, O Lord, are God alone.

I am your servant.

I am not worthy of the least of all the steadfast love and all the faithfulness that you have shown to your servant.

For I know my transgressions,
 and my sin is ever before me.

Woe is me! I am lost, for I am a man of unclean lips.

Wretched man that I am!

I despise myself,
 and repent in dust and ashes.

For your name's sake, O Lord,
 pardon my guilt, for it is great.

God, be merciful to me, a sinner!

I am poor and needy...
 You are my help and my deliverer.

I will praise your righteousness, yours alone.

I am nothing.

May I never boast of anything except the cross.

Ps. 131:1; 2 Kin. 19:19; Ps. 116:16; Gen. 32:10; Ps. 51:3; Is. 6:5; Rom. 7:24; Job 42:6; Ps. 25:11; Luke 18:13; Ps. 70:5; Ps. 71:16; 2 Cor. 12:11; Gal. 6:14 (All verses are from the NRSV.)

The Coming Judgment

Each person is destined to die once and after that comes judgment.

[God] will judge everyone according to what they have done. He will give eternal life to those who keep on doing good, seeking after the glory and honor and immortality that God offers. But he will pour out his anger and wrath on those who live for themselves, who refuse to obey the truth and instead live lives of wickedness.

There will be trouble and calamity for everyone who keeps on doing what is evil....But there will be glory and honor and peace from God for all who do good.

Don't be misled—you cannot mock the justice of God. You will always harvest what you plant. Those who live only to satisfy their own sinful nature will harvest decay and death from that sinful nature. But those who live to please the Spirit will harvest everlasting life from the Spirit.

Remember that the heavenly Father to whom you pray has no favorites. He will judge or reward you according to what you do. So you must live in reverent fear of him during your time as "foreigners in the land."

The time is coming when everything will be revealed; all that is secret will be made public. Whatever you have said in the dark will be heard in the light, and what you have whispered behind closed doors will be shouted from the housetops for all to hear!

Dear friends, don't be afraid of those who want to kill you. They can only kill the body; they cannot do any more to you. But I'll tell you whom to fear. Fear God, who has the power to kill people and then throw them into hell.

Fear God and obey his commands, for this is everyone's duty. God will judge us for everything we do, including every secret thing, whether good or bad.

Heb. 9:27; Rom. 2:6-8; Rom. 2:9-10; Gal. 6:7-8; 1 Pet. 1:17; Luke 12:2-3; Luke 12:4-5; Eccl. 12:13-14
(All verses are from the NLT.)

Your Heavenly Father

You are sons of the LORD your God.

The Father Himself loves you.

Be imitators of God, as dearly loved children.

Be merciful, just as your Father also is merciful.

Be perfect...as your heavenly Father is perfect.

As obedient children, do not be conformed to the desires of your former ignorance. But as the One who called you is holy, you also are to be holy in all your conduct.

Do not despise the LORD's instruction...
   and do not loathe His discipline;
for the LORD disciplines the one He loves,
   just as a father, the son he delights in.

As a father has compassion on his children,
   so the LORD has compassion on those who fear Him.

Your heavenly Father will forgive you.

God...is a father of the fatherless.

All those led by God's Spirit are God's sons....You received the Spirit of adoption, by whom we cry out, "Abba, Father!"

Your Father knows the things you need before you ask Him.

What man among you, if his son asks him for bread, will give him a stone? Or if he asks for a fish, will give him a snake? If you then, who are evil, know how to give good gifts to your children, how much more will your Father in heaven give good things to those who ask Him!

Deut. 14:1; John 16:27; Eph. 5:1; Luke 6:36; Matt. 5:48; 1 Pet. 1:14-15; Prov. 3:11-12; Ps. 103:13; Matt. 6:14; Ps. 68:5; Rom. 8:14-15; Matt. 6:8; Matt. 7:9-11 (All verses are from the HCSB.)

Known By Their Fruits

Little children, let no one deceive you. Whoever practices righteousness is righteous, as [God] is righteous. Whoever makes a practice of sinning is of the devil, for the devil has been sinning from the beginning.

Each tree is known by its own fruit. For figs are not gathered from thornbushes, nor are grapes picked from a bramble bush.

Every healthy tree bears good fruit, but the diseased tree bears bad fruit. A healthy tree cannot bear bad fruit, nor can a diseased tree bear good fruit. Every tree that does not bear good fruit is cut down and thrown into the fire.

Now the works of the flesh are evident: sexual immorality, impurity, sensuality, idolatry, sorcery, enmity, strife, jealousy, fits of anger, rivalries, dissensions, divisions, envy, drunkenness, orgies, and things like these. I warn you, as I warned you before, that those who do such things will not inherit the kingdom of God.

But the fruit of the Spirit is love, joy, peace, patience, kindness, goodness, faithfulness, gentleness, self-control; against such things there is no law. And those who belong to Christ Jesus have crucified the flesh with its passions and desires.

No one born of God makes a practice of sinning, for God's seed abides in him, and he cannot keep on sinning because he has been born of God. By this it is evident who are the children of God, and who are the children of the devil: whoever does not practice righteousness is not of God, nor is the one who does not love his brother.

Everyone who goes on ahead and does not abide in the teaching of Christ, does not have God. Whoever abides in the teaching has both the Father and the Son.

Whoever does good is from God; whoever does evil has not seen God.

1 John 3:7-8; Luke 6:44; Matt. 7:17-19; Gal. 5:19-21; Gal. 5:22-24; 1 John 3:9-10; 2 John 1:9; 3 John 1:11(All verses are from the ESV.)

I Know

I know that the LORD is great,
  and that our Lord is above all gods.
Whatever the LORD pleases, he does,
  in heaven and on earth.

I know that it will be well with those who fear God.

I know that the LORD will maintain the cause of the afflicted,
  and will execute justice for the needy.

This I know, that God is for me.
  In God, whose word I praise,
in the LORD, whose word I praise,
  in God I trust; I shall not be afraid.
What can man do to me?

I know that I shall not be put to shame.
  He who vindicates me is near...
Behold, the Lord GOD helps me;
  who will declare me guilty?

I know whom I have believed, and I am convinced that he is able to guard until
that Day what has been entrusted to me.

I know that my Redeemer lives,
  and at the last he will stand upon the earth.
And after my skin has been thus destroyed,
  yet in my flesh I shall see God,
whom I shall see for myself,
  and my eyes shall behold, and not another.
My heart faints within me!

Ps. 135:5-6; Eccl. 8:12; Ps. 140:12; Ps. 56:9-11; Is. 50:7-9; 2 Tim. 1:12; Job 19.25-27 (All verses
are from the ESV.)

Children of Abraham

God proclaimed...good news to Abraham long ago when he said, "All nations will be blessed through you."

The LORD had said to [him]..."I will make you into a great nation. I will bless you and make you famous, and you will be a blessing to others."

The Scriptures say: "Abraham believed God, and God counted him as righteous because of his faith." He was even called the friend of God.

Even when there was no reason for hope, Abraham kept hoping—believing that he would become the father of many nations. For God had said to him, "That's how many descendants you will have!"

And Abraham's faith did not weaken, even though, at about 100 years of age, he figured his body was as good as dead—and so was Sarah's womb. Abraham never wavered in believing God's promise. In fact, his faith grew stronger, and in this he brought glory to God. He was fully convinced that God is able to do whatever he promises.

And when God counted him as righteous, it wasn't just for Abraham's benefit. It was recorded for our benefit, too, assuring us that God will also count us as righteous if we believe in him, the one who raised Jesus our Lord from the dead.

So the promise is received by faith. It is given as a free gift. And we are all certain to receive it, whether or not we live according to the law of Moses, if we have faith like Abraham's. For Abraham is the father of all who believe.

So all who put their faith in Christ share the same blessing Abraham received.

And now that you belong to Christ, you are the true children of Abraham. You are his heirs, and God's promise to Abraham belongs to you.

Gal. 3:8; Gen. 12:1-2; James 2:23; Rom. 4:18; Rom. 4:19-21; Rom. 4:23-24; Rom. 4:16; Gal. 3:9; Gal. 3:29 (All verses are from the NLT.)

The Son of Man

No one has ascended into heaven, but He who descended from heaven: the Son of Man.

The Son of Man has come to seek and to save that which was lost.

The Son of Man did not come to be served, but to serve, and to give His life a ransom for many.

As Moses lifted up the serpent in the wilderness, even so must the Son of Man be lifted up; so that whoever believes will in Him have eternal life.

The Son of Man is going to be delivered into the hands of men; and they will kill Him, and He will be raised on the third day.

Just as Jonah was three days and three nights in the belly of the sea monster, so will the Son of Man be three days and three nights in the heart of the earth.

All things which are written through the prophets about the Son of Man will be accomplished.

Now is the Son of Man glorified, and God is glorified in Him.

From now on the Son of Man will be seated at the right hand of the power of God.

He gave Him authority to execute judgment, because He is the Son of Man.

For the Son of Man is going to come in the glory of His Father with His angels, and will then repay every man according to his deeds.

Do you believe in the Son of Man?

John 3:13; Luke 19:10; Mark 10:45; John 3:14-15; Matt. 17:22-23; Matt. 12:40; Luke 18:31; John 13:31; Luke 22:69; John 5:27; Matt. 16:27; John 9:35 (All verses are from the NASB.)

Pure Hearts

Who may ascend the mountain of the LORD?
  Who may stand in his holy place?
The one who has clean hands and a pure heart,
  who does not trust in an idol.

The pure in heart...will see God.

Purify your hearts, you double-minded.

Love the LORD your God with all your heart.

In your hearts revere Christ as Lord.

Serve [God] with wholehearted devotion and with a willing mind, for
the LORD searches every heart and understands every desire and every thought.

He knows the secrets of the heart.

The LORD does not look at the things people look at. People look at the outward
appearance, but the LORD looks at the heart.

Above all else, guard your heart,
  for everything you do flows from it.

Store up for yourselves treasures in heaven, where moths and vermin do not
destroy, and where thieves do not break in and steal. For where your treasure is,
there your heart will be also.

May your hearts be fully committed to the LORD our God, to live by his decrees
and obey his commands.

May the Lord...strengthen your hearts so that you will be blameless and holy in
the presence of our God and Father when our Lord Jesus comes.

Ps. 24:3-4; Matt. 5:8; James 4:8; Deut. 6:5; 1 Pet. 3:15; 1 Chr. 28:9; Ps. 44:21; 1 Sam. 16:7;
Prov. 4:23; Matt. 6:20-21; 1 Kin. 8:61; 1 Thess. 3:12-13 (All verses are from the NIV.)

God's Kingdom

The Kingdom of God can't be detected by visible signs. You won't be able to say, "Here it is!" or "It's over there!" For the Kingdom of God is already among you.

The Kingdom of God has arrived.

No one can enter the Kingdom of God without being born of water and the Spirit. Humans can reproduce only human life, but the Holy Spirit gives birth to spiritual life...The wind blows wherever it wants. Just as you can hear the wind but can't tell where it comes from or where it is going, so you can't explain how people are born of the Spirit.

[God] has rescued us from the kingdom of darkness and transferred us into the Kingdom of his dear Son.

He called you to share in his Kingdom.

This same Good News that came to you is going out all over the world.

The Kingdom of Heaven is like a mustard seed planted in a field. It is the smallest of all seeds, but it becomes the largest of garden plants.

You are permitted to understand the secrets of the Kingdom of God.

The Kingdom of God is not just a lot of talk; it is living by God's power.

The Kingdom of God is not a matter of what we eat or drink, but of living a life of goodness and peace and joy in the Holy Spirit.

We are receiving a Kingdom that is unshakable.

All the powers of hell will not conquer it.

Don't be afraid, little flock. For it gives your Father great happiness to give you the Kingdom.

Luke 17:20-21; Matt. 12:28; John 3:5-6, 8; Col.1:13; 1 Thess. 2:12; Col. 1:6; Matt. 13:31-32; Luke 8:10; 1 Cor. 4:20; Rom. 14:17; Heb. 12:28; Matt. 16:18; Luke 12:32 (All verses are from the NLT.)

Save Me, LORD

Lord, I believe.

To you, O LORD, I lift up my soul.

I am poor and needy.

Let your steadfast love come to me, O LORD,
  your salvation according to your promise.

Let your mercy come to me, that I may live.

Draw near to my soul.

Make your face shine on your servant.

In your righteousness bring my soul out of trouble!

You can make me clean.

Blot out my transgressions.

Forgive all my sins.

Let me take refuge under the shelter of your wings!

Be to me a rock of refuge,
  to which I may continually come.

Plead my cause and redeem me;
  give me life according to your promise!

Save me,
  that I may observe your testimonies.

I have trusted in your steadfast love;
  my heart shall rejoice in your salvation.

John 9:38; Ps. 25:1; Ps. 86:1; Ps. 119:41; Ps. 119:77; Ps. 69:18; Ps. 31:16; Ps. 143:11; Luke 5:12; Ps.
51:1; Ps. 25:18; Ps. 61:4; Ps. 71:3; Ps. 119:154; Ps. 119:146; Ps. 13:5 (All verses are from the ESV.)

Taste and See that the LORD Is Good

O taste and see that the LORD is good.

Take delight in the LORD.

He provides food for those who fear him—

spiritual food and...spiritual drink.

Like newborn infants, long for the pure, spiritual milk, so that by it you may grow into salvation—if indeed you have tasted that the Lord is good.

He satisfies the thirsty,
  and the hungry he fills with good things,

    bread from heaven

    and...honey from the rock.

Whoever eats of this bread will live forever.

The LORD of hosts will make for all peoples
  a feast of rich food, a feast of well-aged wines.

People will come from east and west, from north and south, and will eat in the kingdom of God.

Blessed are those who hunger and thirst for righteousness, for they will be filled.

Ps. 34:8; Ps. 37:4; Ps. 111:5; 1 Cor. 10:3-4; 1 Pet. 2:2-3; Ps. 107:9; John 6:32; Ps. 81:16; John 6:51; Is. 25:6; Luke 13:29; Matt. 5:6 (All verses are from the NRSV.)

Friendship

As iron sharpens iron,
  so a friend sharpens a friend.

Two people are better off than one, for they can help each other succeed. If one person falls, the other can reach out and help. But someone who falls alone is in real trouble.

A person standing alone can be attacked and defeated, but two can stand back-to-back and conquer. Three are even better, for a triple-braided cord is not easily broken.

Walk with the wise and become wise;
  associate with fools and get in trouble.

Bad company corrupts good character.

Oh, the joys of those who do not
  follow the advice of the wicked,
or stand around with sinners,
  or join in with mockers.

There are "friends" who destroy each other,
  but a real friend sticks closer than a brother.

The heartfelt counsel of a friend
  is as sweet as perfume and incense.

Never abandon a friend.

A friend is always loyal.

There is no greater love than to lay down one's life for one's friends.

Prov. 27:17; Eccl. 4:9-10; Eccl. 4:12; Prov. 13:20; 1 Cor. 15:33; Ps. 1:1; Prov. 18:24; Prov. 27:9; Prov. 27:10; Prov. 17:17; John 15:13 (All verses are from the NLT.)

Be Subject to
the Government

Let everyone be subject to the governing authorities, for there is no authority except that which God has established. The authorities that exist have been established by God.

Submit yourselves for the Lord's sake to every human authority: whether to the emperor, as the supreme authority, or to governors, who are sent by him to punish those who do wrong and to commend those who do right.

Whoever rebels against the authority is rebelling against what God has instituted, and those who do so will bring judgment on themselves.

Do what is right and you will be commended. For the one in authority is God's servant for your good.

But if you do wrong, be afraid, for rulers do not bear the sword for no reason. They are God's servants, agents of wrath to bring punishment on the wrongdoer. Therefore, it is necessary to submit to the authorities, not only because of possible punishment but also as a matter of conscience.

This is also why you pay taxes, for the authorities are God's servants, who give their full time to governing. Give to everyone what you owe them: If you owe taxes, pay taxes; if revenue, then revenue; if respect, then respect; if honor, then honor.

Give back to Caesar what is Caesar's, and to God what is God's.

Show proper respect to everyone....Fear God, honor the emperor.

I urge...that petitions, prayers, intercession and thanksgiving be made for all people—for kings and all those in authority, that we may live peaceful and quiet lives in all godliness and holiness. This is good, and pleases God our Savior.

Rom. 13:1; 1 Pet. 2:13-14; Rom 13:2; Rom. 13:3-4; Rom. 13:4-5; Rom. 13:6-7; Luke 20:25; 1 Pet. 2:17; 1 Tim. 2:1-3 (All verses are from the NIV.)

GOD SPEAKS:

Be Holy, For I Am Holy

Keep my decrees and follow them. I am the LORD, who makes you holy.

I am God Almighty; walk before me faithfully and be blameless.

These are the things you are to do: Speak the truth to each other, and render true and sound judgment in your courts; do not plot evil against each other, and do not love to swear falsely. I hate all this.

Do not seek revenge or bear a grudge against anyone among your people, but love your neighbor as yourself. I am the LORD.

Show mercy and compassion to one another. Do not oppress the widow or the fatherless, the foreigner or the poor.

For I desire mercy, not sacrifice,
    and acknowledgment of God rather than burnt offerings.

Learn to do right; seek justice.

For I, the LORD, love justice;
    I hate robbery and wrongdoing.

Is not this the kind of fasting I have chosen:
    to loose the chains of injustice
and untie the cords of the yoke,
    to set the oppressed free
and break every yoke?
    Is it not to share your food with the hungry
and to provide the poor wanderer with shelter—
    when you see the naked, to clothe them,
and not to turn away from your own flesh and blood?

Be holy because I, the LORD your God, am holy.

Lev. 20:8; Gen. 17:1; Zech. 8:16-17; Lev. 19:18; Zech. 7:9-10; Hos. 6:6; Is. 1:17; Is. 61:8; Is. 58:6-7; Lev. 19:2 (All verses are from the NIV.)

I Will Praise My God

The LORD is my strength and my song;
  he has given me victory.
This is my God, and I will praise him.

Praise the LORD!
  For he has heard my cry for mercy.
The LORD is my strength and shield.
  I trust him with all my heart.
He helps me, and my heart is filled with joy.
  I burst out in songs of thanksgiving.

I will rejoice in the LORD.
  I will be glad because he rescues me.
With every bone in my body I will praise him.

I will sing to the LORD
  because he is good to me.

I will sing of the LORD's unfailing love forever!

I will always proclaim what God has done.

I will give repeated thanks to the LORD,
  praising him to everyone.
For he stands beside the needy,
  ready to save them from those who condemn them.

Let all that I am praise the LORD;
  with my whole heart, I will praise his holy name.
Let all that I am praise the LORD;
  may I never forget the good things he does for me.

I will sing to the LORD as long as I live.
  I will praise my God to my last breath!

Ex. 15:2; Ps. 28:6-7; Ps. 35:9-10; Ps. 13:6; Ps. 89:1; Ps. 75:9; Ps. 109:30-31; Ps. 103:1-2; Ps. 104:33
(All verses are from the NLT.)

Future Rewards
for the Persecuted

Blessed are those who are persecuted for righteousness' sake, for theirs is the kingdom of heaven.

The one who endures to the end will be saved.

As an example of suffering and patience, beloved, take the prophets who spoke in the name of the Lord. Indeed we call blessed those who showed endurance.

Moses, when he was grown up, refused to be called a son of Pharaoh's daughter, choosing rather to share ill-treatment with the people of God than to enjoy the fleeting pleasures of sin. He considered abuse suffered for the Christ to be greater wealth than the treasures of Egypt, for he was looking ahead to the reward.

Others were tortured....Others suffered mocking and flogging, and even chains and imprisonment. They were stoned to death, they were sawn in two, they were killed by the sword; they went about in skins of sheep and goats, destitute, persecuted, tormented.

All of these died in faith without having received the promises, but from a distance they saw and greeted them. They confessed that they were strangers and foreigners on the earth...They desire a better country, that is, a heavenly one. Therefore God is not ashamed to be called their God; indeed, he has prepared a city for them.

It is through many persecutions that we must enter the kingdom of God.

Let us run with perseverance the race that is set before us, looking to Jesus the pioneer and perfecter of our faith, who for the sake of the joy that was set before him endured the cross, disregarding its shame, and has taken his seat at the right hand of the throne of God.

Let us...bear the abuse he endured.

If we endure, we will also reign with him.

Matt. 5:10; Mark 13:13; James 5:10-11; Heb. 11:24-26; Heb. 11:35-37; Heb. 11:13, 16; Acts 14:22; Heb. 12:1-2; Heb. 13:13; 2 Tim. 2:12 (All verses are from the NRSV.)

How Great You Are

O Lᴏʀᴅ my God, how great you are!

You are ruler of all the kingdoms of the earth.

You rule the oceans.
　You subdue their storm-tossed waves...
The heavens are yours, and the earth is yours;
　everything in the world is yours—you created it all.

You are powerful and mighty; no one can stand against you!

Your right hand, O Lᴏʀᴅ,
　smashes the enemy.
In the greatness of your majesty,
　you overthrow those who rise against you.
You unleash your blazing fury;
　it consumes them like straw.

Everything is possible for you.

Your eternal word, O Lᴏʀᴅ,
　stands firm in heaven.
Your faithfulness extends to every generation,
　as enduring as the earth you created.
Your regulations remain true to this day,
　for everything serves your plans.

O Lᴏʀᴅ, what great works you do!

Let each generation tell its children of your mighty acts;
　let them proclaim your power.

Yours, O Lᴏʀᴅ, is the greatness, the power, the glory, the victory, and the majesty.

Ps. 104:1; 2 Chr. 20:6; Ps. 89:9, 11; 2 Chr. 20:6; Ex. 15:6-7; Mark 14:36; Ps. 119:89-91; Ps. 92:5; Ps. 145:4; 1 Chr. 29:11 (All verses are from the NLT.)

Return to God

Turn from the evil road you are traveling and from the evil things you are doing.

Your sins...have cut you off from God.

Resist the devil, and he will flee from you. Come close to God, and God will come close to you.

As the Scriptures say, "God opposes the proud but favors the humble." So humble yourselves before God.

Do not be stubborn...but submit yourselves to the LORD.

Confess your sin to the LORD.

Let there be tears for what you have done. Let there be sorrow and deep grief. Let there be sadness instead of laughter, and gloom instead of joy.

Don't tear your clothing in your grief,
   but tear your hearts instead.
Return to the LORD your God,
   for he is merciful and compassionate,
slow to get angry and filled with unfailing love.

He will forgive generously.

God blesses those who mourn,
   for they will be comforted.

Stop your sinning and begin to obey the LORD your God.

Jer. 25:5; Is. 59:2; James 4:7-8; James 4:6-7; 2 Chr. 30:8; Ezra 10:11; James 4:9; Joel 2:13; Is. 55:7; Matt. 5:4; Jer. 26:13 (All verses are from the NLT.)

Life Is Fleeting

Human beings...are like a breath;
  their days are like a passing shadow.

All flesh is like grass
  and all its glory like the flower of grass.
The grass withers,
  and the flower falls.

The wind passes over it, and it is gone,
  and its place knows it no more.

You are dust,
  and to dust you shall return.

What is your life? For you are a mist that appears for a little while and then vanishes.

Do not boast about tomorrow,
  for you do not know what a day may bring.

Be careful then how you live, not as unwise people but as wise, making the most
of the time, because the days are evil. So do not be foolish, but understand what
the will of the Lord is.

The days of our life are seventy years,
  or perhaps eighty, if we are strong;
even then their span is only toil and trouble;
  they are soon gone, and we fly away.

We are dust.

Let us not grow weary in doing what is right, for we will reap at harvest time,
if we do not give up. So then, whenever we have an opportunity, let us work for
the good of all, and especially for those of the family of faith.

Ps. 144:3-4; 1 Pet. 1:24; Ps. 103:16; Gen. 3:19; James 4:14; Prov. 27:1; Eph. 5:15-17; Ps. 90:10;
Ps. 103:14; Gal. 6:9-10 (All verses are from the NRSV.)

Set Free From Sin

Everyone who sins is a slave to sin.

At one time we too were foolish, disobedient, deceived and enslaved by all kinds of passions and pleasures. We lived in malice and envy, being hated and hating one another.

We know that our old self was crucified with [Christ] so that the body ruled by sin might be done away with, that we should no longer be slaves to sin— because anyone who has died has been set free from sin.

We were therefore buried with him through baptism into death in order that, just as Christ was raised from the dead through the glory of the Father, we too may live a new life.

Count yourselves dead to sin but alive to God in Christ Jesus.

Do not let sin reign in your mortal body so that you obey its evil desires. Do not offer any part of yourself to sin as an instrument of wickedness, but rather offer yourselves to God as those who have been brought from death to life; and offer every part of yourself to him as an instrument of righteousness.

For sin shall no longer be your master, because you are not under the law, but under grace.

Through Christ Jesus the law of the Spirit who gives life has set you free from the law of sin and death.

So if the Son sets you free, you will be free indeed.

To him who loves us and has freed us from our sins by his blood...to him be glory and power for ever and ever! Amen.

John 8:34; Titus 3:3; Rom. 6:6-7; Rom. 6:4; Rom. 6:11; Rom. 6:12-13; Rom. 6:14; Rom. 8:2; John 8:36; Rev. 1:5-6 (All verses are from the NIV.)

GOD SPEAKS:

You Are Mine

You shall be holy to me, for I the Lord am holy and have separated you from the peoples, that you should be mine.

You are my witnesses,
  and my servant whom I have chosen,
that you may know and believe me
  and understand that I am he....
I am God.

You are my people,

> my chosen,

> my beloved,

> my children,

> my heritage,

> the branch of my planting, the work of my hands,
>   that I might be glorified.

And you are my sheep, human sheep of my pasture.

If you will indeed obey my voice and keep my covenant, you shall be my treasured possession among all peoples...and you shall be to me a kingdom of priests and a holy nation,

you whom I took from the ends of the earth,
  and called from its farthest corners,
saying to you, "You are my servant,
  I have chosen you."

Lev. 20:26; Is. 43:10, 12; Hos. 2:23; Is. 65:9; Jer. 11:15; Is. 45:11; Joel 3:2; Is. 60:21; Ezek. 34:31; Ex. 19:5-6; Is. 41:9 (All verses are from the ESV.)

The Battle Is the LORD's

The battle is the LORD's.

Your God is among you,
a warrior who saves.

The LORD your God is the One who goes with you to fight for you against your enemies to give you victory.

Fear the LORD your God, and He will deliver you from the hand of all your enemies.

No weapon formed against you will succeed.

The LORD will cause the enemies who rise up against you to be defeated before you. They will march out against you from one direction but flee from you in seven directions.

Do not be afraid of them, for the LORD your God...is with you.

The One who is in you is greater than the one who is in the world.

Stand firm and see the LORD's salvation He will provide for you.

The LORD will fight for you.

For the battle is not yours, but God's.

How happy you are, Israel!
Who is like you,
a people saved by the LORD?
He is the shield that protects you,
the sword you boast in.

Victory comes from the LORD.

1 Sam. 17:47; Zeph. 3:17; Deut. 20:4; 2 Kin. 17:39; Is. 54:17; Deut. 28:7; Deut. 20:1; 1 John 4:4; Ex. 14:13; Ex. 14:14; 2 Chr. 20:15; Deut. 33:29; Prov. 21:31 (All verses are from the HCSB.)

Our Savior

We believe that we will be saved through the grace of the Lord Jesus,

who descended from heaven,

who in every respect has been tested as we are, yet without sin,

who was handed over to death for our trespasses,

who...freed us from our sins by his blood,

who was...raised for our justification,

who abolished death and brought life and immortality to light,

who is at the right hand of God,

who indeed intercedes for us,

who rescues us from the wrath that is coming,

who loves us,

who died for us, so that...we may live with him.

Acts 15:11; John 3:13; Heb. 4:15; Rom. 4:25; Rev. 1:5; Rom. 4:25; 2 Tim. 1:10; Rom. 8:34; Rom. 8:34; 1 Thess. 1:10; Rev. 1:5; 1 Thess. 5:10 (All verses are from the NRSV.)

Your Word in My Heart

How can a young person stay pure?
  By obeying your word.
I have tried hard to find you—
  don't let me wander from your commands.
I have hidden your word in my heart,
  that I might not sin against you.

I have followed your commands,
  which keep me from following cruel and evil people.
My steps have stayed on your path;
  I have not wavered from following you.

Your laws please me;
  they give me wise advice.

You have charged us
  to keep your commandments carefully.
Oh, that my actions would consistently
  reflect your decrees!
Then I will not be ashamed
  when I compare my life with your commands.

I will study your commandments
  and reflect on your ways.
I will delight in your decrees
  and not forget your word.

I take joy in doing your will, my God,
  for your instructions are written on my heart.

Ps. 119:9-11; Ps. 17:4-5; Ps. 119:24; Ps. 119:4-6; Ps. 119:15-16; Ps. 40:8 (All verses are from the NLT.)

Be On Guard

Be on guard. Stand firm in the faith. Be courageous. Be strong.

Watch out for your great enemy, the devil. He prowls around like a roaring lion, looking for someone to devour. Stand firm against him, and be strong in your faith.

Stay alert and be clearheaded.

Keep watch and pray, so that you will not give in to temptation. For the spirit is willing, but the body is weak.

If you think you are standing strong, be careful not to fall.

Be on guard so that you will not be carried away by the errors of...wicked people.

False teachers, like vicious wolves, will come in among you...not sparing the flock. Even some men from your own group will rise up and distort the truth in order to draw a following. Watch out!

Watch out for people who cause divisions and upset people's faith by teaching things contrary to what you have been taught. Stay away from them.

Pray in the Spirit at all times and on every occasion. Stay alert.

Beware! Guard against every kind of greed. Life is not measured by how much you own.

Guard your heart above all else,
    for it determines the course of your life.

1 Cor. 16:13; 1 Pet. 5:8-9; 1 Thess. 5:6; Mark 14:38; 1 Cor. 10:12; 2 Pet. 3:17; Acts 20:29-31; Rom. 16:17; Eph. 6:18; Luke 12:15; Prov. 4:23 (All verses are from the NLT.)

Becoming Like Christ

You have stripped off the old self with its practices and have clothed yourselves with the new self, which is being renewed in knowledge according to the image of its creator.

For those whom [God] foreknew he also predestined to be conformed to the image of his Son.

You became imitators...of the Lord.

Whoever says, "I abide in him," ought to walk just as he walked.

Christ...suffered for you, leaving you an example, so that you should follow in his steps.

Just as the Lord has forgiven you, so you also must forgive.

Welcome one another...just as Christ has welcomed you.

And live in love, as Christ loved us.

We must grow up in every way into him,

until all of us come to the unity of the faith and of the knowledge of the Son of God, to maturity, to the measure of the full stature of Christ.

All of us...seeing the glory of the Lord as though reflected in a mirror, are being transformed into the same image from one degree of glory to another.

As was the man of dust, so are those who are of the dust; and as is the man of heaven, so are those who are of heaven. Just as we have borne the image of the man of dust, we will also bear the image of the man of heaven.

What we will be has not yet been revealed. What we do know is this: when he is revealed, we will be like him, for we will see him as he is.

Col. 3:9-10; Rom. 8:29; 1 Thess. 1:6; 1 John 2:6; 1 Pet. 2:21; Col. 3:13; Rom. 15:7; Eph. 5:2; Eph. 4:15; Eph. 4:13; 2 Cor. 3:18; 1 Cor. 15:48-49; 1 John 3:2 (All verses are from the NRSV.)

The Right Path

Give careful thought to your ways.

Give careful thought to the paths for your feet.

Do not set foot on the path of the wicked
   or walk in the way of evildoers.
Avoid it, do not travel on it;
   turn from it and go on your way.

Folly brings joy to one who has no sense,
   but whoever has understanding keeps a straight course.

Let your eyes look straight ahead;
   fix your gaze directly before you...
Do not turn to the right or the left;
   keep your foot from evil.

Devote your heart and soul to seeking the LORD your God.

Walk in the way of insight.

Apply your heart to instruction
   and your ears to words of knowledge.

Pay attention and turn your ear to the sayings of the wise...
   for it is pleasing when you keep them in your heart
and have all of them ready on your lips.

Be wise,
   and set your heart on the right path.

In the way of righteousness there is life;
   along that path is immortality.

The path of the righteous is like the morning sun,
   shining ever brighter till the full light of day.

Hag. 1:7; Prov. 4:26; Prov. 4:14-15; Prov. 15:21; Prov. 4:25, 27; 1 Chr. 22:19; Prov. 9:6; Prov. 23:12; Prov. 22:17-18; Prov. 23:19; Prov. 12:28; Prov. 4:18 (All verses are from the NIV.)

JESUS SPEAKS:

I Will Come Again

You...must be ready, for the Son of Man is coming at an unexpected hour.

When you see the desolating sacrilege standing in the holy place...at that time there will be great suffering, such as has not been from the beginning of the world until now, no, and never will be.

From the fig tree learn its lesson: as soon as its branch becomes tender and puts forth its leaves, you know that summer is near. So also, when you see these things taking place, you know that he is near, at the very gates.

Immediately after the suffering of those days
  the sun will be darkened,
    and the moon will not give its light;
  the stars will fall from heaven,
    and the powers of heaven will be shaken.

Then the sign of the Son of Man will appear in heaven, and then all the tribes of the earth will mourn, and they will see the Son of Man coming on the clouds of heaven with power and great glory. And he will send out his angels with a loud trumpet call, and they will gather his elect from the four winds, from one end of heaven to the other.

Be on guard so that your hearts are not weighed down with dissipation and drunkenness and the worries of this life, and that day does not catch you unexpectedly, like a trap.

Be alert at all times, praying that you may have the strength to escape all these things that will take place, and to stand before the Son of Man.

Do not let your hearts be troubled. Believe in God, believe also in me. In my Father's house there are many dwelling places. If it were not so, would I have told you that I go to prepare a place for you? And if I go and prepare a place for you, I will come again and will take you to myself, so that where I am, there you may be also.

I am coming soon; hold fast to what you have, so that no one may seize your crown.

Luke 12:40; Matt. 24:15, 21; Mark 13:28-29; Matt. 24:29-31; Luke 21:34-35; Luke 21:36; John 14:1-3; Rev. 3:11 (All verses are from the NRSV.)

Glorify God

You who fear the LORD, praise him!
   All you offspring of Jacob, glorify him,
and stand in awe of him, all you offspring of Israel!

Declare his glory among the nations,
   his marvelous works among all the peoples!
For great is the LORD, and greatly to be praised,
   and he is to be feared above all gods.
For all the gods of the peoples are worthless idols,
   but the LORD made the heavens.

The heavens declare the glory of God,
   and the sky above proclaims his handiwork.

Ascribe to the LORD glory and strength!
   Ascribe to the LORD the glory due his name;
bring an offering and come before him!
   Worship the LORD in the splendor of holiness.

There is one God...for whom we exist.

For from him and through him and to him are all things. To him be glory forever.
I appeal to you therefore, brothers, by the mercies of God, to present your bodies
as a living sacrifice, holy and acceptable to God, which is your spiritual worship.

Glorify God in your body.

Whether you eat or drink, or whatever you do, do all to the glory of God.

Live in such harmony with one another, in accord with Christ Jesus, that together
you may with one voice glorify the God and Father of our Lord Jesus Christ.

To him be glory in the church and in Christ Jesus throughout all generations,
forever and ever. Amen.

Ps. 22:23; 1 Chr.16:24-26; Ps. 19:1; 1 Chr. 16:28-29; 1 Cor. 8:6; Rom. 11:36-12:1; 1 Cor. 6:20;
1 Cor. 10:31; Rom. 15:5-6; Eph. 3:21 (All verses are from the ESV.)

Let Us Love One Another

In this the love of God was made manifest among us, that God sent his only Son into the world, so that we might live through him.

If God so loved us, we also ought to love one another.

Let us love one another, for love is from God, and whoever loves has been born of God and knows God.

If we love one another, God abides in us and his love is perfected in us.

Walk in love, as Christ loved us and gave himself up for us, a fragrant offering and sacrifice to God.

By this we know love, that he laid down his life for us, and we ought to lay down our lives for the brothers.

If anyone says, "I love God," and hates his brother, he is a liar; for he who does not love his brother whom he has seen cannot love God whom he has not seen. And this commandment we have from him: whoever loves God must also love his brother.

If anyone has the world's goods and sees his brother in need, yet closes his heart against him, how does God's love abide in him?

Whoever does not love abides in death.

We know that we have passed out of death into life, because we love the brothers.

Let us not love in word or talk but in deed and in truth.

And let us consider how to stir up one another to love and good works.

1 John 4:9; 1 John 4:11; 1 John 4:7; 1 John 4:12; Eph. 5:2; 1 John 3:16; 1 John 4:20-21; 1 John 3:17; 1 John 3:14; 1 John 3:14; 1 John 3:18; Heb. 10:24 (All verses are from the ESV.)

Help Me, Lord

Help me, Lord my God.

Answer me quickly, for I am in trouble.

Hear my cry, O God;
  listen to my prayer.
From the ends of the earth I call to you,
  I call as my heart grows faint;
lead me to the rock that is higher than I.

I rise before dawn and cry for help;
  I have put my hope in your word.

Strengthen me according to your word.

Sustain me, my God, according to your promise.

Lord, my strength and my fortress,
  my refuge in time of distress,

I know that you can do all things;
  no purpose of yours can be thwarted.

When I am in distress, I call to you,
  because you answer me.

Turn to me and have mercy on me;
  show your strength in behalf of your servant.

In your righteousness, bring me out of trouble.

Deliver me, Lord, my faithful God.

Come quickly to help me,
  my Lord and my Savior.

Ps. 109:26; Ps. 69:17; Ps. 61:1-2; Ps. 119:147; Ps. 119:28; Ps. 119:116; Jer. 16:19; Job 42:2; Ps. 86:7; Ps. 86:16; Ps. 143:11; Ps. 31:5; Ps. 38:22 (All verses are from the NIV.)

Dwelling in Safety

The name of the LORD is a strong tower;
  the righteous man runs into it and is safe.

The beloved of the LORD dwells in safety.
  The High God surrounds him all day long,
and dwells between his shoulders.

The steps of a man are established by the LORD,
  when he delights in his way;
though he fall, he shall not be cast headlong,
  for the LORD upholds his hand.

In the day of trouble the LORD delivers him;
  the LORD protects him and keeps him alive;
he is called blessed in the land...
  The LORD sustains him on his sickbed.

He who dwells in the shelter of the Most High
  will abide in the shadow of the Almighty.

He will dwell on the heights;
  his place of defense will be the fortresses of rocks;
his bread will be given him; his water will be sure.

In the fear of the LORD one has strong confidence,
  and his children will have a refuge.

Steadfast love surrounds the one who trusts in the LORD.

Whoever trusts in the LORD is safe.

Prov. 18:10; Deut. 33:12; Ps. 37:23-24; Ps. 41:1-3; Ps. 91:1; Is. 33:16; Prov. 14:26; Ps. 32:10;
Prov. 29:25 (All verses are from the ESV.)

Be Merciful

Be merciful, just as your Father is merciful.

Bear with each other and forgive one another if any of you has a grievance against someone. Forgive as the Lord forgave you.

Be kind and compassionate to one another, forgiving each other, just as in Christ God forgave you.

Do not repay anyone evil for evil....Do not be overcome by evil, but overcome evil with good.

Love your enemies, do good to those who hate you, bless those who curse you, pray for those who mistreat you.

Do not judge, and you will not be judged. Do not condemn, and you will not be condemned. Forgive, and you will be forgiven. Give, and it will be given to you. A good measure, pressed down, shaken together and running over, will be poured into your lap.

For in the same way you judge others, you will be judged, and with the measure you use, it will be measured to you.

For if you forgive other people when they sin against you, your heavenly Father will also forgive you. But if you do not forgive others their sins, your Father will not forgive your sins.

Judgment without mercy will be shown to anyone who has not been merciful. Mercy triumphs over judgment.

Blessed are the merciful,
   for they will be shown mercy.

Luke 6:36; Col. 3:13; Eph. 4:32; Rom. 12:17, 21; Luke 6:27-28; Luke 6:37-38; Matt. 7:2; Matt. 6:14-15; James 2:13; Matt. 5:7 (All verses are from the NIV.)

The Kingdom of God Has Come

The time is fulfilled.

The kingdom of God has come.

The grace of God has appeared, bringing salvation for all people.

The Spirit is poured upon us from on high.

The old has passed away; behold, the new has come.

The light shines in the darkness.

Waters break forth in the wilderness,
  and streams in the desert.

The wilderness becomes a fruitful field,
  and the fruitful field is deemed a forest.

The feeble bind on strength.

The blind receive their sight.

The lame walk.

Lepers are cleansed.

The deaf hear.

The dead are raised up.

And the poor have good news preached to them.

My heart exults in the LORD,

the God who works wonders.

Mark 1:15; Matt.12:28; Titus 2:11; Is. 32:15; 2 Cor. 5:17; John 1:5; Is. 35:6; Is. 32:15; 1 Sam. 2:4; Matt. 11:5; Matt. 11:5; Matt. 11:5; Matt. 11:5; Matt. 11:5; Matt. 11:5; 1 Sam. 2:1; Ps. 77:14 (All verses are from the ESV.)

No One Can Hinder My Plans for You

Listen to me, O house of Jacob,
  all the remnant of the house of Israel,
who have been borne by me from your birth,
  carried from the womb;
even to your old age I am he,
  even when you turn gray I will carry you.
I have made, and I will bear;
  I will carry and will save.

I will save you, and you shall be a blessing.

For surely I know the plans I have for you, plans for your welfare and not for harm, to give you a future with hope.

My purpose shall stand,
  and I will fulfill my intention.

I will build my church, and the gates of Hades will not prevail against it.

I will be a wall of fire all around it.

I am God, and also henceforth I am He;
  there is no one who can deliver from my hand;
I work and who can hinder it?

My sheep hear my voice. I know them, and they follow me. I give them eternal life, and they will never perish. No one will snatch them out of my hand.

Look, I have set before you an open door, which no one is able to shut.

Your hearts will rejoice, and no one will take your joy from you.

Is. 46:3-4; Zech. 8:13; Jer. 29:11; Is. 46:10; Matt. 16:18; Zech. 2:5; Is. 43:13; John 10:27-28; Rev. 3:8; John 16:22 (All verses are from the NRSV.)

Enjoy God's Good Gifts

God...richly gives us all we need for our enjoyment.

The LORD will withhold no good thing
from those who do what is right.

God gives wisdom, knowledge, and joy to those who please him.

From his abundance we have all received one gracious blessing after another.

Whatever is good and perfect comes down to us from God our Father.

God has made everything beautiful for its own time....People should eat and drink and enjoy the fruits of their labor, for these are gifts from God.

These pleasures are from the hand of God. For who can eat or enjoy anything apart from him?

Go ahead. Eat your food with joy, and drink your wine with a happy heart, for God approves of this!

To enjoy your work and accept your lot in life—this is indeed a gift from God.

Rejoice in all you have accomplished because the LORD your God has blessed you.

Celebrate because of all the good things the LORD your God has given to you and your household.

Are...you happy? You should sing praises.

Give thanks to the LORD, for he is good!

1 Tim. 6:17; Ps. 84:11; Eccl. 2:26; John 1:16; James 1:17; Eccl. 3:11, 13; Eccl. 2:24-25; Eccl. 9:7; Eccl. 5:19; Deut. 12:7; Deut. 26:11; James 5:13; 1 Chr. 16:34 (All verses are from the NLT.)

What God Has Done for You

You were called.

You were justified.

You were washed.

You were sanctified.

You were ransomed.

You were sealed.

You...have been taught.

You have been healed.

You have been born again.

You have been raised.

You have been set free.

You have been saved.

Thanks be to God!

1 Cor. 1:9; 1 Cor. 6:11; 1 Cor. 6:11; 1 Cor. 6:11; 1 Pet. 1:18; Eph. 4:30; 1 Thess. 4:9; 1 Pet. 2:24; 1 Pet. 1:23; Col. 3:1; Rom. 6:22; Eph. 2:5; Rom 6:17 (All verses are from the ESV.)

Your Unfailing Love

O LORD, God of Israel, there is no God like you in all of heaven above or on the earth below. You keep your covenant and show unfailing love to all who walk before you in wholehearted devotion.

What are mere mortals that you should think about them,
    human beings that you should care for them?

Who am I, O Sovereign LORD, and what is my family, that you have brought me this far?

I am not worthy of all the unfailing love and faithfulness you have shown to me, your servant.

O Lord, you are so good, so ready to forgive,
    so full of unfailing love for all who ask for your help.

You came when I called;
    you told me, "Do not fear"...
You have redeemed my life.

I will be glad and rejoice in your unfailing love,
    for you have seen my troubles,
and you care about the anguish of my soul.

With all my heart I will praise you, O Lord my God.
    I will give glory to your name forever,
for your love for me is very great.
    You have rescued me from the depths of death.

I will thank you, LORD, among all the people.
    I will sing your praises among the nations.
For your unfailing love is higher than the heavens.
    Your faithfulness reaches to the clouds.

1 Kin. 8:23; Ps. 8:4; 2 Sam. 7:18; Gen. 32:10; Ps. 86:5; Lam. 3:57-58; Ps. 31:7; Ps. 86:12-13; Ps. 108:3-4 (All verses are from the NLT.)

Be Thankful

Be thankful,

always giving thanks to God the Father for everything, in the name of our Lord Jesus Christ.

Enter his gates with thanksgiving
  and his courts with praise;
give thanks to him and praise his name.

Give thanks to the LORD for his unfailing love
  and his wonderful deeds for mankind...
Ponder the loving deeds of the LORD.

Consider what great things he has done for you.

And forget not all his benefits—
  who forgives all your sins
and heals all your diseases,
  who redeems your life from the pit
and crowns you with love and compassion,
  who satisfies your desires with good things
so that your youth is renewed like the eagle's.

Praise the LORD.
  Give thanks to the LORD,

singing to God with gratitude in your hearts. And whatever you do, whether in word or deed, do it all in the name of the Lord Jesus, giving thanks to God the Father through him.

Give thanks in all circumstances; for this is God's will for you in Christ Jesus.

Live your lives in him...overflowing with thankfulness.

Col. 3:15; Eph. 5:20; Ps. 100:4; Ps. 107:21, 43; 1 Sam. 12:24; Ps. 103:2-5; Ps. 106:1; Col. 3:16-17; 1 Thess. 5:18; Col. 2:6-7 (All verses are from the NIV.)

Blessings and Promises

[God's] divine power has granted to us everything pertaining to life and godliness:

>	true knowledge of God's mystery, that is, Christ,

>	forgiveness of our trespasses,

>	fellowship...with the Father, and with His Son,

>	the abundance of grace,

>	the gift of righteousness,

>	the peace of God,

>	the strength of His might,

>	wisdom from above,

>	encouragement in Christ,

>	joy in the Holy Spirit,

>	all the fullness of God.

He has granted to us His precious and magnificent promises:

>	confidence in the day of judgment,

>	victory through our Lord Jesus Christ,

>	a house...in the heavens,

>	an inheritance in the kingdom,

>	eternal glory in Christ.

2 Pet. 1:3; Col. 2:2; Eph. 1:7; 1 John 1:3; Rom. 5:17; Rom. 5:17; Phil. 4:7; Eph. 6:10; James 3:17; Phil. 2:1; Rom. 14:17; Eph. 3:19; 2 Pet. 1:4; 1 John 4:17; 1 Cor. 15:57; 2 Cor. 5:1; Eph. 5:5; 1 Pet. 5:10 (All verses are from the NASB.)

Tell the Good News

Zion, herald of good news,
   go up on a high mountain...
Raise your voice loudly.
   Raise it, do not be afraid!

Go and spread the news of the kingdom of God,

        the good news about Jesus,

        the message of the cross.

Tell the people all about this life.

Report to them how much the Lord has done for you and how He has had
mercy on you.

Don't be ashamed of the testimony about our Lord,

because it is God's power for salvation to everyone who believes.

Proclaim His salvation from day to day.
   Declare His glory among the nations,
His wonderful works among all peoples.

For He has done glorious things.
   Let this be known throughout the earth.

Go...and make disciples of all nations, baptizing them in the name of the Father
and of the Son and of the Holy Spirit.

How beautiful on the mountains
   are the feet of the herald,
who proclaims peace,
   who brings news of good things,
who proclaims salvation.

Is. 40:9; Luke 9:60; Acts 8:35; 1 Cor. 1:18; Acts 5:20; Mark 5:19; 2 Tim. 1:8; Rom. 1:16; Ps. 96:2-3;
Is. 12:5; Matt. 28:19; Is. 52:7 (All verses are from the HCSB.)

JESUS SPEAKS:

The Rewards of Obeying Me

All authority has been given to Me in heaven and on earth. Go, therefore, and make disciples of all nations, baptizing them in the name of the Father and of the Son and of the Holy Spirit, teaching them to observe everything I have commanded you.

The words that I have spoken to you are spirit and are life.

If anyone keeps My word, he will never see death.

If anyone loves Me, he will keep My word. My Father will love him, and We will come to him and make Our home with him.

The one who has My commands and keeps them is the one who loves Me. And the one who loves Me will be loved by My Father. I also will love him and will reveal Myself to him.

You are My friends if you do what I command you.

If you keep My commands you will remain in My love.

Everyone who hears these words of Mine and acts on them will be like a sensible man who built his house on the rock. The rain fell, the rivers rose, and the winds blew and pounded that house. Yet it didn't collapse, because its foundation was on the rock.

If you continue in My word, you really are My disciples. You will know the truth, and the truth will set you free.

If you know these things, you are blessed if you do them.

Matt. 28:18-20; John 6:63; John 8:51; John 14:23; John 14:21; John 15:14; John 15:10; Matt. 7:24-25; John 8:31-32; John 13:17 (All verses are from the HCSB.)

The LORD Is On My Side

This I know, that God is for me.

The LORD is on my side; I will not fear.

Behold, God is my helper;
  the Lord is the upholder of my life.

The Lord GOD helps me...
  and I know that I shall not be put to shame.
He who vindicates me is near.
  Who will contend with me?
Let us stand up together.
  Who is my adversary?
Let him come near to me.
  Behold, the Lord GOD helps me;
who will declare me guilty?

Who shall bring any charge against God's elect? It is God who justifies.

Who is to condemn?

For [God] stands at the right hand of the needy one,
  to save him from those who condemn his soul to death.

I have set the LORD always before me;
  because he is at my right hand, I shall not be shaken.
Therefore my heart is glad, and my whole being rejoices;
  my flesh also dwells secure.

The LORD is on my side as my helper;
  I shall look in triumph on those who hate me.

Ps. 56:9; Ps. 118:6; Ps. 54:4; Is. 50:7-9; Rom. 8:33; Rom. 8:34; Ps. 109:31; Ps. 16:8-9; Ps. 118:7
(All verses are from the ESV.)

The God of All Comfort

The eyes of the LORD are on the righteous,
  and his ears are attentive to their cry...
The LORD is close to the brokenhearted
  and saves those who are crushed in spirit.

The LORD is gracious and compassionate...
  and rich in love.

He heals the brokenhearted
  and binds up their wounds.

God...comforts the downcast.

God...gives endurance and encouragement.

Those who hope in the LORD
  will renew their strength.
They will soar on wings like eagles;
  they will run and not grow weary,
they will walk and not be faint.

The LORD gives strength to his people;
  the LORD blesses his people with peace.

Praise be to the God and Father of our Lord Jesus Christ, the Father of
compassion and the God of all comfort, who comforts us in all our troubles, so
that we can comfort those in any trouble with the comfort we ourselves receive
from God.

May our Lord Jesus Christ himself and God our Father...encourage your hearts
and strengthen you in every good deed and word.

Ps. 34:15, 18; Ps. 145:8; Ps. 147:3; 2 Cor. 7:6; Rom. 15:5; Is. 40:31; Ps. 29:11; 2 Cor. 1:3-4;
2 Thess. 2:16-17 (All verses are from the NIV.)

Give Me Bread from Heaven

LORD...you in your great mercies did not forsake [the people of Israel] in the wilderness.

You gave your good Spirit to instruct them and did not withhold your manna from their mouth.

You gave them bread from heaven.

Morning by morning they gathered it, each as much as he could eat.

Your steadfast love, O LORD, endures forever.

[Your] mercies never come to an end;
   they are new every morning;
great is your faithfulness.

The people of Israel ate the manna forty years.

Forty years you sustained them in the wilderness, and they lacked nothing.

O LORD, you will not restrain
   your mercy from me;
your steadfast love and your faithfulness will
   ever preserve me!

I shall not want.

Feed me with the food that is needful for me,

   the bread of life,

   the true bread from heaven.

Neh. 9:7, 19; Neh. 9:20; Neh. 9:15; Ex. 16:21; Ps. 138:8; Lam. 3:22-23; Ex. 16:35; Neh. 9:21; Ps. 40:11; Ps. 23:1; Prov. 30:8; John 6:35; John 6:32 (All verses are from the ESV.)

Be Content

Take care, and be on your guard against all covetousness, for one's life does not consist in the abundance of his possessions.

Covetousness...is idolatry.

Be content with what you have, for [God] has said, "I will never leave you nor forsake you."

Your Father knows what you need.

The LORD your God has blessed you....The LORD your God has been with you. You have lacked nothing.

You shall not covet your neighbor's wife.

Drink water from your own cistern,
    flowing water from your own well...
Let your fountain be blessed,
    and rejoice in the wife of your youth.

And you shall not desire your neighbor's house, his field, or his male servant, or his female servant, his ox, or his donkey, or anything that is your neighbor's.

You shall rejoice in all the good that the LORD your God has given to you.

Oh, taste and see that the LORD is good!
    Blessed is the man who takes refuge in him!
Oh, fear the LORD, you his saints,
    for those who fear him have no lack!

Those who seek the LORD lack no good thing.

Luke 12:15; Col. 3:5; Heb. 13:5; Matt. 6:8; Deut. 2:7; Deut. 5:21; Prov. 5:15, 18; Deut. 5:21; Deut. 26:11; Ps. 34:8-9; Ps. 34:10 (All verses are from the ESV.)

Angels

Praise the LORD, you angels,
  you mighty ones who carry out his plans,
listening for each of his commands.
  Yes, praise the LORD, you armies of angels
who serve him and do his will!

He sends his angels like the winds,
  his servants like flames of fire.

The angel of the LORD is a guard;
  he surrounds and defends all who fear him.

He will order his angels
  to protect you wherever you go.
They will hold you up with their hands
  so you won't even hurt your foot on a stone.

Don't forget to show hospitality to strangers, for some who have done this have
entertained angels without realizing it!

Jesus...was given a position "a little lower than the angels"; and because he suffered
death for us, he is now "crowned with glory and honor."

Now Christ has gone to heaven. He is seated in the place of honor next to God,
and all the angels and authorities and powers accept his authority.

Don't let anyone condemn you by insisting on...the worship of angels, saying they
have had visions about these things.

Angels are only servants—spirits sent to care for people who will inherit salvation.

Make the LORD of Heaven's Armies holy in your life.
  He is the one you should fear.

Ps. 103:20-21; Heb. 1:7; Ps. 34:7; Ps. 91:11-12; Heb. 13:2; Heb. 2:9; 1 Pet. 3:22; Col. 2:18; Heb. 1:14;
Is. 8:13 (All verses are from the NLT.)

Promises for the Faithful

Draw near to God, and he will draw near to you.

Believe in the LORD your God, and you will be established.

Trust in the LORD with all your heart,
   and do not rely on your own insight.
In all your ways acknowledge him,
   and he will make straight your paths.

Commit your work to the LORD,
   and your plans will be established.

Cast your burden on the LORD,
   and he will sustain you.

Do not say, "I will repay evil";
   wait for the LORD, and he will help you.

Direct your heart to the LORD, and serve him only, and he will deliver you.

Take delight in the LORD,
   and he will give you the desires of your heart.
Commit your way to the LORD;
   trust in him, and he will act.
He will make your vindication shine like the light,
   and the justice of your cause like the noonday.

Humble yourselves before the Lord, and he will exalt you.

Wait for the LORD, and keep to his way,
   and he will exalt you to inherit the land.

James 4:8; 2 Chr. 20:20; Prov. 3:5-6; Prov. 16:3; Ps. 55:22; Prov. 20:22; 1 Sam. 7:3; Ps. 37:4-6;
James 4:10; Ps. 37:34 (All verses are from the NRSV.)

GOD SPEAKS:

Words for the Rebellious

I spread out my hands all the day
  to a rebellious people,
who walk in a way that is not good,
  following their own devices.

Ah, stubborn children,
  who carry out a plan, but not mine,
and who make an alliance, but not of my Spirit,
  that they may add sin to sin.

Listen to me, you stubborn of heart,
  you who are far from righteousness.

Am I a God at hand and not a God far away? Can a man hide himself in secret
places so that I cannot see him? Do I not fill heaven and earth?

I know your sitting down
  and your going out and coming in,
and your raging against me.

Woe to him who strives with him who formed him,
  a pot among earthen pots!

Where were you when I laid the foundation of the earth?
  Tell me, if you have understanding.

Shall a faultfinder contend with the Almighty?
  ...Will you even put me in the wrong?
Will you condemn me that you may be in the right?

Acknowledge your guilt,
  that you rebelled against the LORD your God...
and that you have not obeyed my voice.
  Return, O faithless children,
for I am your master...
  Return, O faithless sons;
I will heal your faithlessness.

Is. 65:2; Is. 30:1; Is. 46:12; Jer. 23:23-24; 2 Kin. 19:27; Is. 45:9; Job 38:4; Job 40:2, 8; Jer. 3:13-
14, 22 (All verses are from the ESV.)

The LORD Provides Food

Who provides food for the ravens
   when their young cry out to God
and wander about in hunger?

Give thanks to the LORD, for he is good!
   ...He gives food to every living thing.

He covers the heavens with clouds,
   provides rain for the earth,
and makes the grass grow in mountain pastures.
   He gives food to the wild animals
and feeds the young ravens when they cry.

Look at the ravens. They don't plant or harvest or store food in barns, for God
feeds them. And you are far more valuable to him than any birds!

So don't worry about these things, saying, "What will we eat? What will we
drink? What will we wear?" These things dominate the thoughts of unbelievers,
but your heavenly Father already knows all your needs. Seek the Kingdom of
God above all else, and live righteously, and he will give you everything you need.

How gracious and merciful is our LORD!
   He gives food to those who fear him;
he always remembers his covenant.

Give thanks to the LORD, for he is good!
   ...For he satisfies the thirsty
and fills the hungry with good things.

Job 38:41; Ps. 136:1, 25; Ps. 147:8-9; Luke 12:24; Matt. 6:31-33; Ps. 111:4-5; Ps. 107:1, 9 (All
verses are from the NLT.)

Be

Be holy.

Be separate.

Be zealous.

Be...courageous.

Be strong in the Lord.

Be steadfast, immovable.

Be self-controlled.

Be patient in tribulation; be constant in prayer.

Be sober-minded; be watchful.

Be wise as serpents and innocent as doves.

Be ready for every good work.

Be kind to one another, tenderhearted.

Be merciful.

Be quick to hear, slow to speak, slow to anger.

Be thankful.

Be content with what you have.

Be glad.

1 Pet. 1:16; 2 Cor. 6:17; Rev. 3:19; Josh. 1:9; Eph. 6:10; 1 Cor. 15:58; 1 Pet. 4:7; Rom. 12:12; 1 Pet. 5:8; Matt. 10:16; Titus 3:1; Eph. 4:32; Luke 6:36; James 1:19; Col. 3:15; Heb. 13:5; Matt. 5:12 (All verses are from the ESV.)

A Prayer for Guidance

I know, O LORD, that a man's way is not in himself,
nor is it in a man who walks to direct his steps.

Teach me the way in which I should walk;
for to You I lift up my soul.

Teach me Your way, O LORD;
I will walk in Your truth.

Make Your way straight before me.

Teach me good discernment and knowledge.

Teach me to do Your will,
for You are my God;
let Your good Spirit lead me on level ground.

Give me understanding, that I may observe Your law
and keep it with all my heart.
Make me walk in the path of Your commandments,
for I delight in it.

O God, You have taught me from my youth.

Teach me, O LORD, the way of Your statutes,
and I shall observe it to the end.

For Your name's sake You will lead me and guide me.

You will make known to me the path of life.

You have taken hold of my right hand.
With Your counsel You will guide me,
and afterward receive me to glory.

Lead me in the everlasting way.

Jer. 10:23; Ps. 143:8; Ps. 86:11; Ps. 5:8; Ps. 119:66; Ps. 143:10; Ps. 119:34-35; Ps. 71:17; Ps. 119:33; Ps. 31:3; Ps. 16:11; Ps. 73:23-24; Ps. 139:24 (All verses are from the NASB.)

Jesus Is Eternal

[Jesus said], "Very truly I tell you, before Abraham was born, I am!"

He was with God in the beginning.

He was chosen before the creation of the world, but was revealed in these last times.

[Jesus] became flesh and made his dwelling among us.

When [he] had offered for all time one sacrifice for sins, he sat down at the right hand of God.

We know that since Christ was raised from the dead, he cannot die again; death no longer has mastery over him.

[He] has become a priest not on the basis of a regulation as to his ancestry but on the basis of the power of an indestructible life.

Because Jesus lives forever, he has a permanent priesthood. Therefore he is able to save completely those who come to God through him, because he always lives to intercede for them.

Jesus...will come back.

[He] will transform our lowly bodies so that they will be like his glorious body.

And so we will be with the Lord forever.

Jesus Christ is the same yesterday and today and forever.

John 8:58; John 1:2; 1 Pet. 1:20; John 1:14; Heb. 10:12; Rom. 6:9; Heb. 7:16; Heb. 7:24-25; Acts 1:11; Phil. 3:21; 1 Thess. 4:17; Heb. 13:8 (All verses are from the NIV.)

May the LORD *Bless You*

May the LORD your God be with you.

May the LORD...show you kindness and faithfulness.

May the name of the God of Jacob protect you.

May the LORD answer you when you are in distress.

May the LORD give you discretion and understanding.

May the LORD reward you well.

May he give you the desire of your heart
 and make all your plans succeed.

The LORD bless you
 and keep you;
the LORD make his face shine on you
 and be gracious to you;
the LORD turn his face toward you
 and give you peace.

Josh. 1:17; 2 Sam. 2:6; Ps. 20:1; Ps. 20:1; 1 Chr. 22:12; 1 Sam. 24:19; Ps. 20:4; Num. 6:24-26
(All verses are from the NIV.)

Hope in God, My Soul

I remember my affliction and my wandering,
  the bitterness and the gall.
I well remember them,
  and my soul is downcast within me.
Yet this I call to mind
  and therefore I have hope:
Because of the LORD's great love we are not consumed,
  for his compassions never fail.
They are new every morning.

Why, my soul, are you downcast?
  Why so disturbed within me?
Put your hope in God,
  for I will yet praise him,
my Savior and my God.

Yes, my soul, find rest in God;
  my hope comes from him.
Truly he is my rock and my salvation;
  he is my fortress, I will not be shaken.

I say to myself, "The LORD is my portion;
  therefore I will wait for him."
The LORD is good to those whose hope is in him,
  to the one who seeks him.

March on, my soul; be strong!

Praise the LORD, my soul,
  and forget not all his benefits.

Praise the LORD.
  Praise the LORD, my soul.

Lam. 3:19-23; Ps. 42:5; Ps. 62:5-6; Lam. 3:24-25; Judges 5:21; Ps. 103:2; Ps. 146:1 (All verses are from the NIV.)

GOD SPEAKS:

I Am With You

Thus says the high and lofty one
　who inhabits eternity, whose name is Holy:
I dwell in the high and holy place,
　and also with those who are contrite and humble in spirit,
to revive the spirit of the humble,
　and to revive the heart of the contrite.

I am with you and will bless you.

Do not fear, for I am with you,
　do not be afraid, for I am your God;
I will strengthen you, I will help you,
　I will uphold you with my victorious right hand.

I will walk among you, and will be your God, and you shall be my people.

My presence will go with you, and I will give you rest.

Know that I am with you and will keep you wherever you go.

When you pass through the waters, I will be with you;
　and through the rivers, they shall not overwhelm you;
when you walk through fire you shall not be burned,
　and the flame shall not consume you.

Do not be afraid...
　for I am with you to deliver you

I will be with you; I will not fail you or forsake you.

My spirit abides among you; do not fear.

Is. 57:15; Gen. 26:24; Is. 41:10; Lev. 26:12; Ex. 33:14; Gen. 28:15; Is. 43:2; Jer. 1:8; Josh. 1:5;
Hag. 2:5 (All verses are from the NRSV.)

What Is Promised to You

You died to this life, and your real life is hidden with Christ in God.

Your names are registered in heaven.

God's Holy Spirit...has identified you as his own, guaranteeing that you will be saved on the day of redemption.

God is protecting you by his power until you receive this salvation, which is ready to be revealed on the last day.

You have to endure many trials for a little while. These trials will show that your faith is genuine....So when your faith remains strong through many trials, it will bring you much praise and glory and honor on the day when Jesus Christ is revealed to the whole world.

And when Christ, who is your life, is revealed to the whole world, you will share in all his glory.

Then God will give you a grand entrance into the eternal Kingdom of our Lord and Savior Jesus Christ.

He will lift you up in honor.

The Lord will give you an inheritance as your reward,

an inheritance that is kept in heaven for you, pure and undefiled, beyond the reach of change and decay.

And the LORD himself...will live among you!

He will take delight in you with gladness.
   With his love, he will calm all your fears.
He will rejoice over you with joyful songs.

Patient endurance is what you need now, so that you will continue to do God's will. Then you will receive all that he has promised.

Col. 3:3; Luke 10:20; Eph. 4:30; 1 Pet. 1:5; 1 Pet. 1:6-7; Col. 3:4; 2 Pet. 1:11; 1 Pet. 5:6; Col 3:24; 1 Pet. 1:4; Zeph. 3:15; Zeph. 3:17; Heb. 10:36 (All verses are from the NLT.)

Our Sins Are Forgiven

Our sins testify against us...
  and we know our iniquities:
transgressing, and denying the LORD,
  and turning back from following our God.

But...we have an advocate with the Father, Jesus Christ the righteous. He is the propitiation for our sins.

Everyone who believes in him receives forgiveness of sins through his name.

He himself bore our sins in his body on the tree, that we might die to sin and live to righteousness.

He was pierced for our transgressions;
  he was crushed for our iniquities;
upon him was the chastisement that brought us peace,
  and with his wounds we are healed.
All we like sheep have gone astray;
  we have turned—every one—to his own way;
and the LORD has laid on him
  the iniquity of us all,

having forgiven us all our trespasses, by canceling the record of debt that stood against us with its legal demands. This he set aside, nailing it to the cross.

He does not deal with us according to our sins,
  nor repay us according to our iniquities.
For as high as the heavens are above the earth,
  so great is his steadfast love toward those who fear him;
as far as the east is from the west,
  so far does he remove our transgressions from us.

The blood of Jesus his Son cleanses us from all sin.

Is. 59:12-13; 1 John 2:1-2; Acts 10:43; 1 Pet. 2:24; Is. 53:5-6; Col. 2:13-14; Ps. 103:10-12; 1 John 1:7
(All verses are from the ESV.)

For Your Sake
I Bear Reproach

O LORD...know that for your sake I bear reproach.

My foes are vigorous, they are mighty,
  and many are those who hate me wrongfully.
Those who render me evil for good
  accuse me because I follow after good.

They drop trouble upon me,
  and in anger they bear a grudge against me.

My soul is in the midst of lions...
  the children of man, whose teeth are spears and arrows,
whose tongues are sharp swords.

Wicked and deceitful mouths are opened against me,
  speaking against me with lying tongues.
They encircle me with words of hate,
  and attack me without cause.
In return for my love they accuse me,
  but I give myself to prayer.

You have seen the wrong done to me, O LORD...
  You have seen all their vengeance,
all their plots against me.
  You have heard their taunts.

Vindicate me, O God, and defend my cause
  against an ungodly people.

Contend, O LORD, with those who contend with me!

O GOD my Lord,
  deal on my behalf for your name's sake...
Let them know that this is your hand;
  you, O LORD, have done it!
Let them curse, but you will bless!

Jer. 15:15; Ps. 38:19-20; Ps. 55:3; Ps. 57:4; Ps. 109:2-4; Lam. 3:59-61; Ps. 43:1; Ps. 35:1; Ps. 109:21, 27-28 (All verses are from the ESV.)

Is Anything Too Hard for the LORD?

Is anything too hard for the LORD?

Have you not known? Have you not heard?
  The LORD is the everlasting God,
the Creator of the ends of the earth.
  He does not faint or grow weary.

Great is our Lord, and abundant in power;
  his understanding is beyond measure.
The LORD lifts up the humble;
  he casts the wicked to the ground.

The LORD kills and brings to life;
  he brings down to Sheol and raises up.

And God raised the Lord and will also raise us up by his power.

With God all things are possible.

Ah, Lord GOD! It is you who has made the heavens and the earth by your great power and by your outstretched arm!

You are the God who works wonders;
  you have made known your might among the peoples.

Was it not you who dried up the sea,
  the waters of the great deep,
who made the depths of the sea a way
  for the redeemed to pass over?

I know that you can do all things.

Nothing is too hard for you.

Gen. 18:14; Is. 40:28; Ps. 147:5-6; 1 Sam. 2:6; 1 Cor. 6:14; Matt. 19:26; Jer. 32:17; Ps. 77:14; Is. 51:10; Job 42:2; Jer. 32:17 (All verses are from the ESV.)

True Religion
Summarized

He has told you, O man, what is good;
  and what does the LORD require of you
But to do justice, to love kindness,
  and to walk humbly with your God?

This is His commandment, that we believe in the name of His Son Jesus Christ, and love one another, just as He commanded us.

"You shall love the Lord your God with all your heart, and with all your soul, and with all your mind." This is the great and foremost commandment. The second is like it, "You shall love your neighbor as yourself." On these two commandments depend the whole Law and the Prophets.

Love does no wrong to a neighbor; therefore love is the fulfillment of the law.

Pure and undefiled religion in the sight of our God and Father is this: to visit orphans and widows in their distress, and to keep oneself unstained by the world.

Now, Israel, what does the LORD your God require from you, but to fear the LORD your God, to walk in all His ways and love Him, and to serve the LORD your God with all your heart and with all your soul, and to keep the LORD's commandments and His statutes?

The conclusion, when all has been heard, is: fear God and keep His commandments, because this applies to every person.

Mic. 6:8; 1 John 3:23; Matt. 22:37-40; Rom. 13:10; James 1:27; Deut. 10:12-13; Eccl. 12:13 (All verses are from the NASB.)

Controlling the Tongue

If anyone thinks he is religious without controlling his tongue, then his religion is useless and he deceives himself.

My dearly loved brothers, understand this: Everyone must be quick to hear, slow to speak.

Life and death are in the power of the tongue.

There is...a time to be silent.

A gossip goes around revealing a secret,
    but a trustworthy person keeps a confidence.

Whoever conceals an offense promotes love,
    but whoever gossips about it separates friends.

There is...a time to speak.

A word spoken at the right time
    is like gold apples on a silver tray.

The mind of the righteous person thinks before answering,
    but the mouth of the wicked blurts out evil things.

There is one who speaks rashly,
    like a piercing sword;
but the tongue of the wise brings healing.

Pleasant words are a honeycomb:
    sweet to the taste and health to the body.

No foul language is to come from your mouth, but only what is good for building up someone in need, so that it gives grace to those who hear.

When there are many words, sin is unavoidable,
    but the one who controls his lips is wise.

James 1:26; James 1:19; Prov. 18:21; Eccl. 3:1, 7; Prov. 11:13; Prov. 17:9; Eccl. 3:1, 7; Prov. 25:11; Prov. 15:28; Prov. 12:18; Prov. 16:24; Eph. 4:29; Prov. 10:19 (All verses are from the HCSB.)

I Give Eternal Life

I am the resurrection and the life.

Anyone who believes in me will live, even after dying.

Those who drink the water I give will never be thirsty again. It becomes a fresh, bubbling spring within them, giving them eternal life.

I tell you the truth, those who listen to my message and believe in God who sent me have eternal life. They will never be condemned for their sins, but they have already passed from death into life.

I tell you the truth, anyone who obeys my teaching will never die!

My sheep listen to my voice; I know them, and they follow me. I give them eternal life, and they will never perish. No one can snatch them away from me.

As Moses lifted up the bronze snake on a pole in the wilderness, so the Son of Man must be lifted up, so that everyone who believes in him will have eternal life. For God loved the world so much that he gave his one and only Son, so that everyone who believes in him will not perish but have eternal life.

For it is my Father's will that all who see his Son and believe in him should have eternal life. I will raise them up at the last day.

Everyone who lives in me and believes in me will never ever die. Do you believe this?

John 11:25; John 11:25; John 4:14; John 5:24; John 8:51; John 10:27-28; John 3:14-16; John 6:40; John 11:26 (All verses are from the NLT.)

The LORD *Is...*

The LORD is the everlasting God,
   the Creator of the ends of the earth,

> the Ancient of Days,

> the LORD of hosts,

> the Mighty One of Jacob,

> the Holy One of Israel.

God is the King,

> the blessed and only Sovereign,

> the Majesty on high,

> the Father of glory,

> the Judge of all.

The LORD is the strength of his people,

> the Rock,

> the saving refuge of his anointed,

> the Redeemer,

> the fountain of living waters,

> the hope of all the ends of the earth
>   and of the farthest seas.

Is. 40:28; Dan. 7:9; Zeph. 2:9; Is. 49:26; Is. 41:14; Ps. 47:7; 1 Tim. 6:15; Heb. 1:3; Eph. 1:17; Heb. 12:23; Ps. 28:8; Deut. 32:4; Ps. 28:8; Is. 49:7; Jer. 2:13; Ps. 65:5 (All verses are from the ESV.)

Waiting for Jesus to Return

The grace of God...teaches us to say "No" to ungodliness and worldly passions, and to live self-controlled, upright and godly lives in this present age, while we wait for the blessed hope—the appearing of the glory of our great God and Savior, Jesus Christ.

Our citizenship is in heaven. And we eagerly await a Savior from there, the Lord Jesus Christ, who, by the power that enables him to bring everything under his control, will transform our lowly bodies so that they will be like his glorious body.

We...groan inwardly as we wait eagerly for our adoption to sonship, the redemption of our bodies. For in this hope we were saved. But hope that is seen is no hope at all. Who hopes for what they already have? But if we hope for what we do not yet have, we wait for it patiently.

Be patient, then, brothers and sisters, until the Lord's coming. See how the farmer waits for the land to yield its valuable crop, patiently waiting for the autumn and spring rains. You too, be patient and stand firm,

until the day dawns and the morning star rises in your hearts.

In just a little while,
   he who is coming will come
and will not delay.

With minds that are alert and fully sober, set your hope on the grace to be brought to you when Jesus Christ is revealed at his coming.

Be dressed ready for service and keep your lamps burning, like servants waiting for their master to return from a wedding banquet, so that when he comes and knocks they can immediately open the door for him. It will be good for those servants whose master finds them watching when he comes.

Keep yourselves in God's love as you wait for the mercy of our Lord Jesus Christ to bring you to eternal life.

Titus 2:11-13; Phil. 3:20-21; Rom. 8:23-25; James 5:7-8; 2 Pet. 1:19; Heb. 10:37; 1 Pet. 1:13; Luke 12:35-37; Jude 1:21 (All verses are from the NIV.)

You Alone Are God

O LORD the God of Israel, who are enthroned above the cherubim, you are God, you alone, of all the kingdoms of the earth.

You are great and do wondrous things;
　you alone are God.

What god in heaven or on earth can perform deeds and mighty acts like yours!

From ages past no one has heard,
　no ear has perceived,
no eye has seen any God besides you,
　who works for those who wait for him.
You meet those who gladly do right,
　those who remember you.

Those who worship vain idols
　forsake their true loyalty.

But I trust in you, O LORD;
　I say, "You are my God."

Whom have I in heaven but you?
　And there is nothing on earth that I desire other than you.

O LORD...to you shall the nations come
　from the ends of the earth and say:
Our ancestors have inherited nothing but lies,
　worthless things in which there is no profit.
Can mortals make for themselves gods?
　Such are no gods!

There is no God besides you.

Blessed be your glorious name, which is exalted above all blessing and praise....
You are the LORD, you alone.

2 Kin. 19:15; Ps. 86:10; Deut. 3:24; Is. 64:4-5; Jon. 2:8; Ps. 31:14; Ps. 73:25; Jer. 16:19-20;
2 Sam. 7:22; Neh. 9:5-6 (All verses are from the NRSV.)

Justified by Faith

Who may ascend into the hill of the LORD?
   And who may stand in His holy place?
He who has clean hands and a pure heart.

Who among us can live with the consuming fire?
   Who among us can live with continual burning?
He who walks righteously.

Shall we be saved?
   For all of us have become like one who is unclean,
and all our righteous deeds are like a filthy garment.

For all have sinned and fall short of the glory of God.

By the works of the Law no flesh will be justified in His sight.

There is none righteous, not even one.

But now apart from the Law the righteousness of God has been manifested...the righteousness of God through faith in Jesus Christ for all those who believe.

[God] made Him who knew no sin to be sin on our behalf, so that we might become the righteousness of God in Him.

Having been justified by faith, we have peace with God through our Lord Jesus Christ.

For Christ...died for sins once for all, the just for the unjust, so that He might bring us to God.

We have confidence to enter the holy place by the blood of Jesus....Let us draw near with a sincere heart in full assurance of faith.

Ps. 24:3-4; Is. 33:14-15; Is. 64:5-6; Rom. 3:23; Rom. 3:20; Rom. 3:10; Rom. 3:21-22; 2 Cor. 5:21; Rom. 5:1; 1 Pet. 3:18; Heb. 10:19, 22 (All verses are from the NASB.)

God's Armor

Defend the faith that God has entrusted once for all time to his holy people.

We are not fighting against flesh-and-blood enemies, but against evil rulers and authorities of the unseen world, against mighty powers in this dark world, and against evil spirits in the heavenly places.

We are human, but we don't wage war as humans do. We use God's mighty weapons, not worldly weapons, to knock down the strongholds of human reasoning and to destroy false arguments.

Be strong in the Lord and in his mighty power.

Put on all of God's armor so that you will be able to stand firm against all strategies of the devil.

Stand your ground, putting on the belt of truth and the body armor of God's righteousness.

For shoes, put on the peace that comes from the Good News so that you will be fully prepared.

In addition to all of these, hold up the shield of faith to stop the fiery arrows of the devil.

Put on salvation as your helmet, and take the sword of the Spirit, which is the word of God.

Let us who live in the light be clearheaded, protected by the armor of faith and love, and wearing as our helmet the confidence of our salvation.

Put on every piece of God's armor so you will be able to resist the enemy in the time of evil. Then after the battle you will still be standing firm.

For every child of God defeats this evil world, and we achieve this victory through our faith.

Jude 1:3; Eph. 6:12; 2 Cor. 10:3-4; Eph. 6:10; Eph. 6:11; Eph. 6:14; Eph. 6:15; Eph. 6:16; Eph. 6:17; 1 Thess. 5:8; Eph. 6:13; 1 John 5:4 (All verses are from the NLT.)

The Messiah Is Coming

Every valley shall be lifted up,
  and every mountain and hill be made low;
the uneven ground shall become level,
  and the rough places a plain.
And the glory of the LORD shall be revealed,
  and all flesh shall see it together,
for the mouth of the LORD has spoken.

There shall come forth a shoot from the stump of Jesse,
  and a branch from his roots shall bear fruit.
And the Spirit of the LORD shall rest upon him,
  the Spirit of wisdom and understanding,
the Spirit of counsel and might,
  the Spirit of knowledge and the fear of the LORD.
And his delight shall be in the fear of the LORD.

He will tend his flock like a shepherd;
  he will gather the lambs in his arms;
he will carry them in his bosom,
  and gently lead those that are with young.

In that day the deaf shall hear
  the words of a book,
and out of their gloom and darkness
  the eyes of the blind shall see.

Then shall the lame man leap like a deer,
  and the tongue of the mute sing for joy.

The meek shall obtain fresh joy in the LORD,
  and the poor among mankind shall exult in the Holy One of Israel.

Is. 40:4-5; Is. 11:1-3; Is. 40:11; Is. 29:18; Is. 35:6; Is. 29:19 (All verses are from the ESV.)

The Child to Be Born

Rejoice greatly....Your king comes to you!

Bethlehem Ephrathah,
   though you are small among the clans of Judah,
out of you will come...
   one who will be ruler over Israel,
whose origins are from of old,
   from ancient times.

The virgin will conceive and give birth to a son, and they will call him Immanuel (which means "God with us").

The holy one to be born will be called the Son of God.

You are to give him the name Jesus, because he will save his people from their sins.

In his name the nations will put their hope.

The rising sun will come to us from heaven
   to shine on those living in darkness
and in the shadow of death,
   to guide our feet into the path of peace.

For to us a child is born,
   to us a son is given,
and the government will be on his shoulders.
   And he will be called
Wonderful Counselor, Mighty God,
   Everlasting Father, Prince of Peace.

The Lord God will give him the throne of his father David, and he will reign over Jacob's descendants forever; his kingdom will never end.

The zeal of the LORD Almighty
   will accomplish this.

Zech. 9:9; Mic. 5:2; Matt. 1:23; Luke 1:35; Matt. 1:21; Matt. 12:21; Luke 1:78-79; Is. 9:6; Luke 1:32-33; Is. 9:7 (All verses are from the NIV.)

God With Us

I bring you good news that will cause great joy for all the people. Today in the town of David a Savior has been born to you; he is the Messiah, the Lord.

God has come to help his people.

Jesus Christ has come in the flesh.

The Son of God has come and has given us understanding, so that we may know him who is true.

No one has ever seen God, but the one and only Son, who is himself God and is in closest relationship with the Father, has made him known.

For God was pleased to have all his fullness dwell in him.

We have seen his glory, the glory of the one and only Son, who came from the Father, full of grace and truth.

This grace was given us in Christ Jesus before the beginning of time, but it has now been revealed through the appearing of our Savior.

The Father has sent his Son to be the Savior of the world.

Praise be to the Lord, the God of Israel,
  because he has come to his people and redeemed them.

Glory to God in the highest heaven,
  and on earth peace to those on whom his favor rests.

Luke 2:10-11; Luke 7:16; 1 John 4:2; 1 John 5:20; John 1:18; Col. 1:19; John 1:14; 2 Tim. 1:9-10; 1 John 4:14; Luke 1:68; Luke 2:14 (All verses are from the NIV.)

Your Will Be Done On Earth

My eyes shed streams of tears
 because your law is not kept.

Justice is turned back,
 and righteousness stands at a distance;
for truth stumbles in the public square,
 and uprightness cannot enter.

Destruction and violence are before me;
 strife and contention arise.

On every side the wicked prowl,
 as vileness is exalted among humankind.

Rise up, O God, judge the earth.

Let the evil of the wicked come to an end.

Because of their many transgressions cast them out,
 for they have rebelled against you.

But establish the righteous.

Let all who take refuge in you rejoice;
 let them ever sing for joy.

Let the skies rain down righteousness.

Let justice roll down like waters,
 and righteousness like an ever-flowing stream.

Let your glory be over all the earth.

Your kingdom come.
 Your will be done,
on earth as it is in heaven.

Ps. 119:136; Is. 59:14; Hab. 1:3; Ps. 12:8; Ps. 82:8; Ps. 7:9; Ps. 5:10; Ps. 7:9; Ps. 5:11; Is. 45:8; Amos 5:24; Ps. 108:5; Matt. 6:10 (All verses are from the NRSV.)

Wait for Me

Wait for me,
  for the day I will stand up to testify.
I have decided to assemble the nations,
  to gather the kingdoms
and to pour out my wrath on them—
  all my fierce anger.

I will contend with those who contend with you.

See, I will defend your cause
  and avenge you.

It is mine to avenge; I will repay.
  In due time their foot will slip;
their day of disaster is near
  and their doom rushes upon them.

But for you who revere my name, the sun of righteousness will rise with healing
in its rays. And you will go out and frolic like well-fed calves. Then you will
trample on the wicked; they will be ashes under the soles of your feet on the day
when I act.

I am bringing my righteousness near,
  it is not far away;
and my salvation will not be delayed.

Shout and be glad, Daughter Zion. For I am coming, and I will live among you.

Then you will know that I am the Lord;
  those who hope in me will not be disappointed.

Zeph. 3:8; Is. 49:25; Jer. 51:36; Deut. 32:35; Mal. 4:2-3; Is. 46:13; Zech. 2:10; Is. 49:23 (All
verses are from the NIV.)

You Will Weep No More

Blessed are you who weep now,
  for you will laugh.

Weeping may stay for the night,
  but rejoicing comes in the morning.

The night is nearly over; the day is almost here.

The LORD will surely comfort Zion

and...bestow on [those who grieve] a crown of beauty
  instead of ashes,
the oil of joy
  instead of mourning,
and a garment of praise
  instead of a spirit of despair.

Those who sow with tears
  will reap with songs of joy.
Those who go out weeping,
  carrying seed to sow,
will return with songs of joy,
  carrying sheaves with them.

They will enter Zion with singing;
  everlasting joy will crown their heads.
Gladness and joy will overtake them,
  and sorrow and sighing will flee away.

The Sovereign LORD will wipe away the tears
  from all faces.

The LORD will be your everlasting light,
  and your days of sorrow will end.

You will weep no more.

Luke 6:21; Ps. 30:5; Rom. 13:12; Is. 51:3; Is. 61:3; Ps. 126:5-6; Is. 35:10; Is. 25:8; Is. 60:20;
Is. 30:19 (All verses are from the NIV.)

Awake

Awake, O sleeper,
  and arise from the dead,
and Christ will shine on you.

An hour is coming, and is now here, when the dead will hear the voice of the Son of God, and those who hear will live.

For the Lord himself will descend from heaven with a cry of command, with the voice of an archangel, and with the sound of the trumpet of God. And the dead in Christ will rise first.

In Christ shall all be made alive....What is raised is imperishable....It is raised in glory....It is raised in power.

Awake, awake,
  put on your strength, O Zion;
put on your beautiful garments...
  Shake yourself from the dust and arise.

You were sealed for the day of redemption.

The day dawns and the morning star rises in your hearts.

Behold, the Lord comes with ten thousands of his holy ones.

And he will send out his angels with a loud trumpet call, and they will gather his elect from the four winds, from one end of heaven to the other.

We...will be caught up together...in the clouds to meet the Lord in the air, and so we will always be with the Lord.

For God has not destined us for wrath, but to obtain salvation through our Lord Jesus Christ, who died for us so that whether we are awake or asleep we might live with him.

You who dwell in the dust, awake and sing for joy!

Eph. 5:14; John 5:25; 1 Thess. 4:16; 1 Cor. 15:22, 42-43; Is. 52:1-2; Eph. 4:30; 2 Pet. 1:19; Jude 1:14; Matt. 24:31; 1 Thess. 4:17; 1 Thess. 5:9-10; Is. 26:19 (All verses are from the ESV.)

Let All Creation Rejoice

Shout for joy, you heavens!
  Earth, rejoice!
Mountains break into joyful shouts!
  For the LORD has comforted His people,
and will have compassion on His afflicted ones.

All the trees of the forest will shout for joy
  before the LORD, for He is coming—
for He is coming to judge the earth.
  He will judge the world with righteousness
and the peoples with His faithfulness.

See, the Lord GOD comes with strength,
  and His power establishes His rule.

Hallelujah, because our Lord God, the Almighty,
  has begun to reign!

Sing a new song to the LORD;
  sing to the LORD, all the earth.

Let the heavens be glad and the earth rejoice,
  and let them say among the nations, "The LORD is King!"
Let the sea and everything in it resound;
  let the fields and all that is in them exult.

Let the rivers clap their hands;
  let the mountains shout together for joy.

The heavens proclaim His righteousness;
  all the peoples see His glory.

All the ends of the earth
  have seen our God's victory.

Shout triumphantly to the LORD, all the earth.

Is. 49:13; Ps. 96:12-13; Is. 40:10; Rev. 19:6; Ps. 96:1; 1 Chr. 16:31-32; Ps. 98:8; Ps. 97:6; Ps. 98:3;
Ps. 100:1 (All verses are from the HCSB.)

Eternal Victory

It is done.

Death has been swallowed up in victory.

No longer will there be any curse.

The creation itself will be liberated from its bondage to decay and brought into the freedom and glory of the children of God.

There will be no more death or mourning or crying or pain, for the old order of things has passed away.

Look! God's dwelling place is now among the people, and he will dwell with them.

The throne of God and of the Lamb will be in the city,

the paradise of God.

Nothing impure will ever enter it...but only those whose names are written in the Lamb's book of life.

And the leaves of the tree [of life] are for the healing of the nations....Blessed are those who wash their robes, that they may have the right to the tree of life and may go through the gates into the city.

They will see [God's] face, and his name will be on their foreheads.

There will be no more night. They will not need the light of a lamp or the light of the sun, for the Lord God will give them light. And they will reign for ever and ever.

Those who are victorious will inherit all this.

Thanks be to God! He gives us the victory through our Lord Jesus Christ.

Rev. 21:6; 1 Cor. 15:54; Rev. 22:3; Rom. 8:21; Rev. 21:4; Rev. 21:3; Rev. 22:3; Rev. 2:7; Rev. 21:27; Rev. 22:2, 14; Rev. 22:4; Rev. 22:5; Rev. 21:7; 1 Cor. 15:57 (All verses are from the NIV.)

Acknowledgments

My deepest thanks to these wonderful people for their prayers, suggestions, and support throughout the years of this project: David, John, and Matthew Rutledge; Amy and Isaiah McPeak; David and Beverly Ralston; Scott and Cindy Ralston; Mary Houk and Connie Massie.

References Used

Roget's Thesaurus of the Bible by A. Colin Day, published by Castle Books in 2003 (currently out of print, but available online at *www.colinday.co.uk*)

Zondervan NIV Nave's Topical Bible, edited by John R. Kohlenberger III, published by Zondervan in 1992

www.BibleGateway.com

www.ESVBible.org

For more on the
daily devotions in this book
visit LightForEachDay.com

LYNN RUTLEDGE

LIGHT FOR EACH DAY

DAILY DEVOTIONS CONTAINING
ONLY THE WORDS OF THE BIBLE | VOLUME 1

Light for Each Day, Volume 1
available at Amazon.com
and other booksellers